Microsoft Access 97 Projects

Harry L. Phillips
Stan Dobrawa

Santa Rosa Junior College

COURSE
TECHNOLOGY

ONE MAIN STREET, CAMBRIDGE, MA 02142

an International Thomson Publishing company I⊤P®

Cambridge • Albany • Bonn • Boston • Cincinnati • London • Madrid • Melbourne • Mexico City
New York • Paris • San Francisco • Singapore • Tokyo • Toronto • Washington

Microsoft® Access 97 — Illustrated Projects™

is published by Course Technology.

Managing Editor:	Nicole Jones Pinard
Product Manager:	Jeanne Herring
Production Editor:	Roxanne Alexander
Composition House:	GEX, Inc.
Quality Assurance Tester:	Chris Hall
Text Designer:	Joseph Lee Design
Cover Designer:	Joseph Lee Design

© 1997 by Course Technology
A Division of International Thomson Publishing — I T P®

For more information contact:

Course Technology
One Main Street
Cambridge, MA 02142

International Thomson Publishing Europe
Berkshire House 168-173
High Holborn
London WC1V 7AA
England

Thomas Nelson Australia
102 Dodds Street
South Melbourne, 3205
Victoria, Australia

Nelson Canada
1120 Birchmount Road
Scarborough, Ontario
Canada M1K 5G4

International Thomson Editores
Campos Eliseos 385, Piso 7
Col. Polanco
11560 Mexico D.F. Mexico

International Thomson Publishing GmbH
Königswinterer Strasse 418
53277 Bonn
Germany

International Thomson Publishing Asia
211 Henderson Road
#05-10 Henderson Building
Singapore 0315

International Thomson Publishing Japan
Hirakawacho Kyowa Building, 3F
2-2-1 Hirakawacho
Chiyoda-ku, Tokyo 102
Japan

Trademarks

Course Technology and the Open Book logo are registered trademarks of Course Technology.
Illustrated Projects and the Illustrated Series are trademarks of Course Technology.

I T P® The ITP logo is a registered trademark of International Thomson Publishing.

Some of the product names and company names used in this book have been used for identification purposes only and may be trademarks or registered trademarks of their respective manufacturers and sellers.

Disclaimer

Course Technology reserves the right to revise this publication and make changes from time to time in its content without notice.

ISBN 0-7600-5131-3

Printed in the United States of America

10 9 8 7 6 5 4 3 2 1

From the Illustrated Series™ Team

At Course Technology we believe that technology will transform the way that people teach and learn. We are very excited about bringing you, instructors and students, the most practical and affordable technology-related products available.

The Development Process

Our development process is unparalleled in the educational publishing industry. Every product we create goes through an exacting process of design, development, review, and testing.

Reviewers give us direction and insight that shape our manuscripts and bring them up to the latest standards. Every manuscript is quality tested. Students whose backgrounds match the intended audience work through every keystroke, carefully checking for clarity and pointing out errors in logic and sequence. Together with our own technical reviewers, these testers help us ensure that everything that carries our name is as error-free and easy to use as possible.

The Products

We show both how and why technology is critical to solving problems in the classroom and in whatever field you choose to teach or pursue. Our time-tested, step-by-step instructions provide unparalleled clarity. Examples and applications are chosen and crafted to motivate students.

The Illustrated Series Team

The Illustrated Series Team is committed to providing you with the most visual introduction to microcomputer applications. No other series of books will get you up to speed faster in today's changing software environment. This book will suit your needs because it was delivered quickly, efficiently, and affordably. In every aspect of business, we rely on a commitment to quality and the use of technology. Each member of the Illustrated Series Team contributes to this process. The names of all our team members are listed below.

Cynthia Anderson	Mary-Terese Cozzola	Meta Hirschl	Gregory Schultz
Chia-Ling Barker	Carol M. Cram	Jane Hosie-Bounar	Ann Shaffer
Donald Barker	Kim Crowley	Steven Johnson	Dan Swanson
David Beskeen	Catherine G. DiMassa	Bill Lisowski	Marie Swanson
Ann Marie Buconjic	Stan Dobrawa	Tara O'Keefe	Jennifer Thompson
Rachel Bunin	Shelley Dyer	Harry Phillips	Sasha Vodnik
Joan Carey	Linda Eriksen	Nicole Jones Pinard	Jan Weingarten
Patrick Carey	Jessica Evans	Katherine T. Pinard	Christie Williams
Sheralyn Carroll	Lisa Friedrichsen	Kevin Proot	Janet Wilson
Pat Coleman	Michael Halvorson	Elizabeth Eisner Reding	
Brad Conlin	Jamie Harper	Art Rotberg	
Pam Conrad	Jeanne Herring	Neil Salkind	

Preface

Welcome to *Microsoft Access 97—Illustrated Projects*. This highly visual book offers a wide array of interesting and challenging projects designed to reinforce the skills learned in any beginning Access book. The Illustrated Projects Series is for people who want more opportunities to practice important software skills.

Organization and Coverage

This text contains a total of six units. Each unit contains three projects followed by four Independent Challenges and a Visual Workshop. In these units, students practice creating different types of databases as well as custom reports that present selected database information in a useful way.

About this Approach

What makes the Illustrated Projects approach so effective at reinforcing software skills? It's quite simple. Each activity in a project is presented on two facing pages, with the step-by-step instructions on the left page, and large screen illustrations on the right. Students can focus on a single activity without having to turn the page. This unique design makes information extremely accessible and easy to absorb. Students can complete the projects on their own and because of the modular structure of the book, can also cover the units in any order.

Each two-page spread, or "information display," contains the following elements:

Road map—It is always clear which project and activity you are working on.

Introduction—Concise text that introduces the project and explains which activity within the project the student will complete. Procedures are easier to learn when they fit into a meaningful framework.

Tips for Microsoft Access 7 users—The steps and figures in this book feature Microsoft Access 97. However, the two software releases are *very* similar. Where there are differences, specific steps are given.

Hints and Trouble comments—Hints for using Microsoft Access 97 more effectively and troubleshooting advice to fix common problems that might occur. Both appear right where students need them, next to the step where they might need help.

Numbered steps—Clear step-by-step directions explain how to complete the specific activity. These steps get less specific as students progress to the third project in a unit.

Time To checklists—Reserved for basic skills that students should do frequently, such as previewing, printing, saving, and closing worksheets.

Clues to Use Boxes—Many activities feature these sidebars, providing concise information that either explains a skill or concept that is covered in the steps or describes an independent task or feature that is in some way related to the steps. These often include both text and screen shots.

Access 97

PROJECT 3

OVERVIEW

Marine Circumnavigation Records

As an avid sailor, it has always been your dream to get into the record books by single-handedly circumnavigating the globe in a sailboat. You want to accomplish this in a way that no other human has before. In researching this ambitious project, you have learned that for your trip to be accepted as a true circumnavigation, you must pass through two antipodal points that are at least 12,429 stature miles apart. You have also gathered a list of data regarding past circumnavigation accomplishments and would like to compile this list into usable information. To do so, you will design and input a **database table, query the table,** and then **create a report**.

activities:

Create the Database, Queries, and Report

Access 7 Users

Click the Table View button on the Design View toolbar to switch to Datasheet View.

Hint

You can use the asterisk (*) wildcard character to match any number or character. The asterisk wildcard can be used as the first or last character in the character string you are searching.

Time To
✓ Save
✓ Close

steps:

1. Create a database called **Circumnavigations**, then create a table named **Records** as shown in Figure P3-1

2. Enter the data as shown in Figure P3-2
   Your table should match the one shown in Figure P3-2. After reviewing your entries, you have noticed some errors that you need to correct.

3. Locate and change the vessel named **Victoria** to **Vittoria**, the sailor named **Albert Cowan** to **Albert Gowan**, and the End Date **5/10/1969** to **5/10/1960**

4. Using **Simple Query Wizard**, create a query named **Solos Records Query** that shows all fields from the Records table except **ID** and displays only those records whose Category field contains the word **solo**

5. Modify the query to sort in ascending order by **End Date**

6. Save and close the query

7. Using **Report Wizard**, create a custom report named **Solo Records Report** as shown in Figure P3-3, using the Solo Records query, do not group or sort the report, use a Tabular Layout, a Landscaped orientation, adjust the field widths so all fields fit on a page, and a corporate style

Clues to Use

Using wildcards

You can use wildcards to search for partial or matching values. The asterisk (*) wildcard can be used to match any number of characters and can be used as the last or first characters in a character(s) string. For example, wh* *would find* what, while, *and* why; *on* *would find* on, sony, only *and* wonder; *and* *ee *would find* see, knee, *and* glee.

The Projects

The two-page lesson format featured in this book provides students with a powerful learning experience. Additionally, this book contains the following features:

► **Meaningful Examples**—This book features projects that students will be excited to create, including a database of unblended coffees, a subscriber mailing list, and an employee roster. By producing relevant documents that will enhance their own lives, students will more readily master skills.

► **Different Levels of Guidance**—the three projects in each unit provide varying levels of guidance. In Project 1, the guidance level is high, with detailed instructions keeping the student on track. Project 2 provides less guidance, and Project 3 provides minimal help, encouraging students to work more independently. This approach gets students in the real-world mindset of using their experiences to solve problems.

► **Start from Scratch**—To truly test if a student understands the software and can use it to reach specific goals, the student should start from scratch. This adds to the book's flexibility and real-world nature.

► **Outstanding Assessment and Reinforcement**—Each unit concludes with four Independent Challenges. These Independent Challenges offer less instruction than the projects, allowing students to explore various software features and increase their critical thinking skills. The Visual Workshop follows the Independent Challenges and broadens students' attention to detail. Students see a completed report, and must recreate it on their own.

Access 97

FIGURE P3-1: Design View of Records table

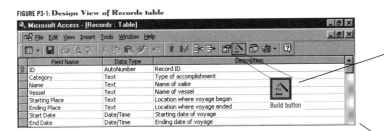

Callouts and enlarged buttons–The innovative design draws the students' eyes to important areas of the screen.

Screen shots–Every activity features large representations of what the screen should look like as students complete the numbered steps.

FIGURE P3-2: Data records 1 to 12 or the Records table

ID	Category	Name	Vessel	Starting Place	Ending Place	Start Date	End Date
1	Earliest	Juan Sebastian	Victoria	Seville, Spain	San Lucar, Spain	9/20/1519	9/6/1521
2	Earliest Woman	Bare	Etoile	St. Malo, France	St. Malo, France	7/12/1766	10/3/1769
3	Earliest Yacht	Lord/Lady Brassey	Sunbeam	Isle of Wight, England	Isle of Wight, England	4/25/1876	7/10/1877
4	Earliest Solo	Jashua Slocum	Spray	Newport, USA	Newport, USA	4/24/1895	7/3/1898
5	Earliest Motor	Albert Cowen	Speedjacks	New York, USA	New York, USA	3/10/1921	5/14/1922
6	Earliest Woman Solo	Krystyna Chojnowska	Mazurek	Las Palmas, USA	Tied Knot, USA	3/28/1976	3/21/1978
7	Smallest Boat	Hiroshi Aoki	Ahdori II	Osaka, Japan	Osaka, Japan	6/12/1972	7/29/1974
8	Earliest Submarine	Edward Beach	USS Triton	New London, USA	New London, USA	2/16/1960	5/10/1969
9	Fastest Solo	Alain Colas	Manureva	St. Malo, France	St. Malo, France	9/28/1993	3/29/1994
10	Fastest	Mike Gill	Great Britain II	Thames, England	Thames, England	8/31/1975	10/9/1975
11	Fastest Solo	Kenichi Horie	Mermaid III	Osaka, Japan	Osaka, Japan	8/1/1973	5/5/1974
12	Earliest Non-stop Solo	Robin Knox	Suhaili	Falmouth, England	Falmouth, England	6/14/1968	4/22/1969

FIGURE P3-3: Solo Records report

Solo Records Report

Category	*Name*	*Vessel*	*Starting Place/Date*		*Ending Place/Date*	
Earliest Solo	Jashua Slocum	Spray	Newport, USA	4/24/1895	Newport, USA	7/3/1898
Earliest Woman Solo	Krystyna Chojnowsk	Mazurek	Las Palmas, USA	3/28/1976	Tied Knot, USA	3/21/1978
Fastest Solo	Alain Colas	Manureva	St. Malo, France	9/28/1993	St. Malo, France	3/29/1994
Fastest Solo	Kenichi Horie	Mermaid III	Osaka, Japan	8/1/1973	Osaka, Japan	5/5/1974
Earliest Non-stop Solo	Robin Knox	Suhaili	Falmouth, England	6/14/1968	Falmouth, England	4/22/1969

Completed report–At the end of every project, there is a picture of how the report will look when printed. Students can easily assess how well they've done.

PERSONAL DATABASES ACD-19

Instructor's Resource Kit

The Instructor's Resource Kit is Course Technology's way of putting the resources and information needed to teach and learn effectively into your hands. With an integrated array of teaching and learning tools that offer you and your students a broad range of instructional options, we believe this kit represents the highest quality and most cutting edge resources available to instructors today. Visit us on the Web at http://www.course.com. Briefly, the resources available with this text are:

Course Faculty Online Companion

This new World Wide Web site offers Course Technology customers a password-protected Faculty Lounge where you can find everything you need to prepare for class. These periodically updated items include lesson plans, graphic files for the figures in the text, additional problems, updates and revisions to the text, links to other Web sites, and access to Student Disk files. This new site is an ongoing project and will continue to evolve throughout the semester. Contact your Customer Service Representative for the site address and password.

Course Student Online Companion

The Student Online Companion is a place where students can access challenging, engaging, and relevant exercises. They can find a graphical glossary of terms found in the text, an archive of meaningful templates, software, hot tips, and Web links to other sites that contain pertinent information. We offer student sites in the broader application areas as well as sites for specific titles. These new sites are also ongoing projects and will continue to evolve throughout the semester.

Instructor's Manual

This is quality assurance-tested and includes:
► *Solutions to end-of-unit material*
► *Lecture notes which contain teaching tips from the author*
► *Extra Projects*

Clues to Use

The Illustrated Family of Products

This book that you are holding fits into the Illustrated Projects Series—*one series of three in the* Illustrated family of products. *The other two series are the* Illustrated Series *and the* Illustrated Interactive Series. *The* Illustrated Series *consists of concepts and applications texts that offer the quickest, most visual way to* build software skills. *The* Illustrated Interactive Series *is our line of computer-based training multimedia products that offer the novice user a quick, visual, and interactive learning experience. All three series are committed to providing you and your students with the most visual and enriching instructional materials.*

Contents

Microsoft
► Access
Projects

Product and Service Databases

In This Unit You Will Create A:

 ► **Product Database**

 ► **Equipment Maintenance Schedule**

 ► **Service Schedule**

Companies of all sizes use product or service databases to track the products or services they provide their customers or use to maintain a business. Product databases typically include a product ID, product name, product description, unit price, selling price, and supplier code. These databases also may track the number of units in stock, a minimum number to keep in stock, and the number on order. Service databases typically track detailed information on the type of service provided by the business. For example, an environmental restoration firm might create a database that tracks information on completed and ongoing restoration projects, such as project name, project type, contractor, contact, project bid, project cost, project timelines, and other project details. ►In this unit you will learn how to use Microsoft Access to create and work with product databases and service databases. You will create relational and non-relational database tables with the Table Wizard and Design View, apply simple and advanced filters, work with calculated fields, create queries with one or more conditions, and create custom reports.

Unblended Coffees Database for Exotic Imports, Inc.

Melanie Cercos, the owner of Exotic Imports, purchases exotic coffees, teas, and spices for sale in her store in New York City. To provide customers with information on specific types of coffees grown in specific regions of the world, she asks you to do the following:

Project Activities

Create a Relational Database

You will create a relational database that includes an Unblended Coffees table and a Ratings table. The Unblended Coffees table will include the name of the coffee, the country of origin, and a numerical rating Melanie assigns to each type of coffee based on its taste and its rareness. The Ratings table will include this numerical rating plus a short description of each rating.

Apply Simple and Advanced Filters

Next, you will apply filters to the Unblended Coffees table to select coffees by a rating or by country of origin, so that you can provide this information to customers.

Create a Select Query

You will use the Query Wizard to create a Select Query that includes fields from the two Unblended Coffees and Ratings tables, so that you can gather information from both into one report.

Prepare and Print a Custom Report

You will update the query by changing the criteria to select only coffees produced in the Caribbean or South America. Then you will use the Report Wizard to produce and print a custom report.

When you have completed Project 1, the custom report will appear as shown in Figure P1-1.

South American Coffees

Coffee	Country	Quality
Barahona	Dominican Republic	Excellent
Blue Mountain	Jamaica	Unique
High Mountain	Jamaica	Outstanding
Jamaican Mountain Choice	Jamaica	Excellent
Medellin	Colombia	Outstanding
Merida	Venezuela	Unique
Pluma	Mexico	Excellent
Tachira	Venezuela	Excellent
Vintage Colombian	Colombia	Unique

activity:

Create a Relational Database

Melanie Cercos wants you to create a relational database for Exotic Imports that includes a table of unblended coffee varieties and a ratings table. In the Unblended Coffees table, you will include the name of the unblended coffee, the country which produces the coffee, and a quality rating. The Ratings table will include a list of all the ratings Melanie uses, plus the meaning of each rating.

steps:

1. Start Microsoft Access, then create a database named **Exotic Imports** on the disk where you plan to save all the files for this book

   Since the Unblended Coffees table will be similar to product tables used by other businesses, you decide to use the Table Wizard to create the table.

2. In the Exotic Imports: Database window, click the **Tables tab** (if necessary), click **New**, click **Table Wizard** in the New Table dialog box, click **OK**, then click **Products** in the Sample Tables list

   For this product table, you need ID, unblended coffee name, country of origin, and rating fields.

3. Double-click **ProductID** in the Sample Fields list to add this field name to the Fields in the my new table list box, click **Rename Field**, type **ID**, then press **[Enter]**; add the **ProductName** field and rename it **Coffee**, add the **ProductDescription** field and rename it **Country**, and add the **CategoryID** field and rename it **Rating**

   Your table now contains four fields. Next, name the table and set the primary key.

4. Click **Next**, type **Unblended Coffees** in the table name box, click the **Yes, set a primary key for me option button** (if necessary), click **Next**, click the **Enter data directly into the table option button** (if necessary), then click **Finish**

   Access automatically sets the ID field as the primary key. Now you're ready to enter information on the coffee products carried by Exotic Imports.

5. Maximize the Unblended Coffees: Table window, then enter the name, country of origin, and rating for each of the 18 unblended coffees, as shown in Figure P1-2, then close the Unblended Coffees table

   Now you're ready to create the Ratings table. Again, you can use the Table Wizard and fields from the Products sample table.

6. In the Tables sheet, click **New**, double-click **Table Wizard** in the New Table dialog box, click **Products** in the Sample Tables list, double-click **ProductID**, rename it **Rating**, double-click **ProductDescription**, rename it **Quality**, then click **Next**; type **Ratings** in the table name box, click the **Yes, set a primary key for me option button** (if necessary), then click **Next**

   The Table Wizard now allows you to define a relationship between the Ratings and Unblended Coffees tables. By defining a relationship on a field found in two different tables, such as Rating, you can produce queries and reports that display meaningful information instead of codes.

7. Click **Relationships**, then in the Relationships dialog box, click **One record in the 'Ratings' table will match many records in the Unblended Coffees' table option button**, click **OK**, then click **Next**

   After you define a one-to-many relationship between the Ratings and Unblended Coffees table, you are ready to enter data into the new Ratings table.

8. Click the **Enter data directly into the table option button** (if necessary), click **Finish**, then use Figure P1-3 to enter the rating and quality information

9. Close the Ratings table and save any changes you have made to the layout of the Ratings table

   You have successfully created the two tables that constitute the Exotic Imports database.

Hint

If you click a field name in the Sample Fields list box, then click the Add Single Field button ▸ , Access adds the field name to the Fields in my new table list box.

Hint

If you cannot see a long entry in a field, double-click the border between fields to automatically adjust the field width. You can use the same technique to narrow the width of fields with short entries.

...

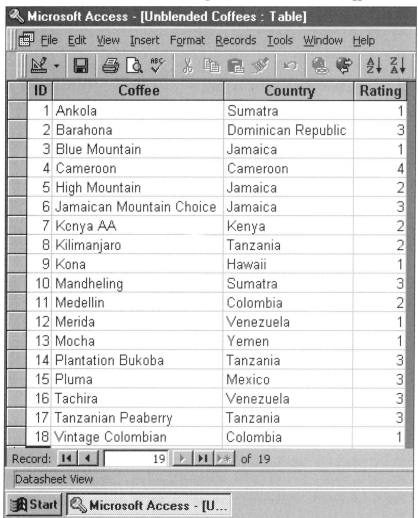

FIGURE P1-2: Data records 1 to 18 for the Unblended Coffees table

ID	Coffee	Country	Rating
1	Ankola	Sumatra	1
2	Barahona	Dominican Republic	3
3	Blue Mountain	Jamaica	1
4	Cameroon	Cameroon	4
5	High Mountain	Jamaica	2
6	Jamaican Mountain Choice	Jamaica	3
7	Kenya AA	Kenya	2
8	Kilimanjaro	Tanzania	2
9	Kona	Hawaii	1
10	Mandheling	Sumatra	3
11	Medellin	Colombia	2
12	Merida	Venezuela	1
13	Mocha	Yemen	1
14	Plantation Bukoba	Tanzania	3
15	Pluma	Mexico	3
16	Tachira	Venezuela	3
17	Tanzanian Peaberry	Tanzania	3
18	Vintage Colombian	Colombia	1

Record: 19 of 19

Datasheet View

FIGURE P1-3: Data records 1 to 5 for the Ratings table

Rating	Quality
1	Unique
2	Outstanding
3	Excellent
4	Good
5	Fair
Number	

Clues to Use

Using Copy and Paste to enter data

If you need to enter the same information repeatedly, such as the same country name, you can use copy and paste. Simply select the data you want to copy, click the Copy button on the Table Datasheet toolbar, click the field in the record to which you want to copy the entry, then click the Paste button.

activity:

Apply Simple and Advanced Filters

Now that you have created the Unblended Coffees table, you can quickly respond to customer inquiries about coffees from specific countries by filtering the table. Using the same techniques, you also can inform customers of highly rated coffees and can answer questions about where specific coffees are grown. You can even perform more advanced filters where you specify more than one condition. A customer calls from Boston and wants to know which coffees Exotic Imports carries from Tanzania. You decide to open the Unblended Coffees table and filter it using the customer's criterion.

steps:

1. In the Microsoft Access Database window, open the **Unblended Coffees** table, right-click **Tanzania** in the Country field of record 8, then click **Filter by Selection** on the shortcut menu

Access displays three records where the entry in the Country field is Tanzania. You tell the customer that the store carries three blends of coffees from Tanzania: Kilimanjaro, Plantation Bukoba, and Tanzanian Peaberry. The next customer that calls asks you which coffees are your top-rated blends.

2. Click the **Remove Filter button** on the Table Datasheet toolbar, right-click **1** in the Rating field of record 1, then click **Filter by Selection** on the shortcut menu

Access shows those records where the entry in the Ratings field is 1. You provide this information to the customer. Later in the day, a customer in the store wants to know what blends you carry from Cameroon and Yemen. To locate this information, you need to use an advanced filter.

3. Click the **Remove Filter button** , click **Records** on the menu bar, point to **Filter**, click **Advanced Filter/Sort**

Access shows a Fields List box for the Unblended Coffees table and a Design grid for specifying the conditions for a filter. You want to clear the grid so that you can specify a new condition.

4. After Design View opens, click **Edit** on the menu bar, then click **Clear Grid**

Because you want to filter the table by country, you need to add the Country field to the Design grid, then specify the conditions.

5. Double-click **Country** in the Fields List box, enter **Yemen** in the first Criteria cell under the Country field, then enter **Cameroon** in the next Criteria cell, which is labeled "or"

Your criteria should match those shown in Figure P1-4. By placing the two conditions in two different Criteria cells, you created an OR condition. Access will select records that meet either condition.

6. Click the **Apply Filter button** on the Filter/Sort toolbar

Microsoft Access shows two records on blends that meet the conditions you specified: the Cameroon and Mocha blends. A new customer wants to know which coffees carry the two top ratings from Melanie. You need to remove the current filter so that you can create a new advanced filter. In addition to selecting blends with a rating of 1 or 2, you want to arrange the results in order by Coffee name.

7. Click the **Remove Filter button** on the Table Datasheet toolbar, click **Records** on the menu bar, point to **Filter**, click **Advanced Filter/Sort**, and after Design View opens, click **Edit** on the menu bar, then click **Clear Grid**

Now you are ready to specify the conditions and the order of the selected records for the advanced filter.

8. Double-click the **Coffee** field in the Fields List box, click the **Sort cell** under the Coffee field, click the **Sort list arrow**, then click **Ascending**; double-click the **Rating** field name in the Field Lists box, click the **Criteria cell** below the Rating field, type **1 or 2**, then click the **Apply Filter button** on the Filter/Sort toolbar

Access shows information on 10 coffees that Melanie considers either "Unique" or "Outstanding," as shown in Figure P1-5.

9. Click the **Remove Filter button** on the Query Datasheet toolbar, then close the table

Hint

Maximize the Design View window so that you can see the entire grid.

Hint

You could achieve the same results by entering the condition "Yemen" Or "Cameroon" in the first Criteria cell.

Hint

Note that Access automatically places quotation marks around each of your criteria.

FIGURE P1-4: Criteria for selecting Yemen or Cameroon

Unblended Coffees
Fields list box

OR condition

Design grid

Criteria cells

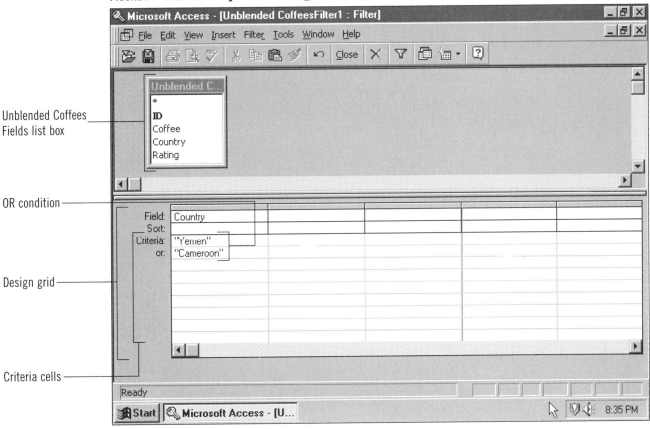

FIGURE P1-5: Access displays coffees with a Rating of 1 or 2, and lists the coffees in order by name

Coffees listed in
alphabetical order

Coffees with a
Rating of 1 or 2

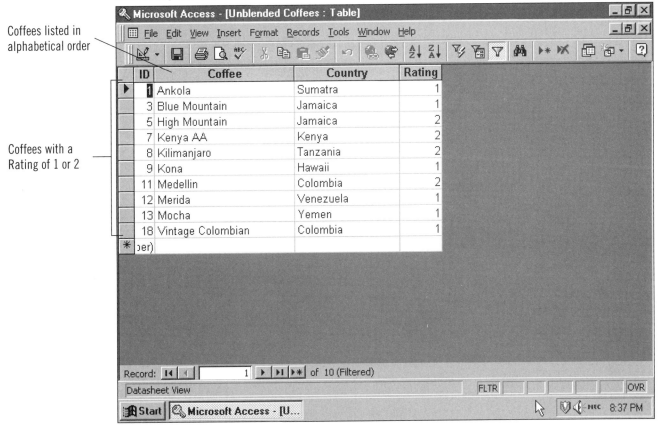

PROJECT 1

UNBLENDED COFFEES DATABASE FOR EXOTIC IMPORTS, INC.

activity:

Create a Select Query

Melanie wants you to prepare a report that lists unblended coffees produced in the Caribbean and South America. She wants the final report to include the name, country, and quality of each coffee. To produce this report, you decide to create a query that includes fields from both the Unblended Coffees and Ratings tables, then you can update the query to select only South American coffees.

steps:

1. Click the **Queries tab**, click **New**, then in the New Query dialog box, double-click **Simple Query Wizard**

Next, from the Simple Query Wizard dialog box, select the first table and the fields from that table that you want to include in your query.

2. Click the **Tables/Queries list arrow**, click **Table: Unblended Coffees**, double-click **Coffee** in the Available Fields list box, then double-click **Country**

Access adds these two fields from the Unblended Coffees to the Selected Fields list box. Now, you can add the Quality field from the other table.

3. Click the **Tables/Queries list arrow**, click **Table: Ratings**, double-click **Quality** in the Available Fields list box, then click **Next**

Next, name and then view your query.

4. Type **South American Coffees** in the Query name box, click the **Open the query to view information option button** (if necessary), then click **Finish**

Access shows the coffee names and countries of origin from the Unblended Coffees table and the corresponding Quality from the Ratings table, as shown in Figure P1-6. Now you can revise the query to include only coffees from South America.

Hint

If the View button shows the icon for Design View (the default), you can just click the button to switch to Design View. If you click the View button's list arrow, then you can choose the type of view you want from a menu.

5. Click the **View button** on the Query Datasheet toolbar

Access switches to Query Design View. You see Field list boxes for both tables, plus the link you established earlier between the Ratings field in each table. In the Design grid, you see the three fields from the two tables. Next, you want to specify the names of the countries to include in the report.

6. In the Design grid, click the first **Criteria cell** below the Country field, type **Colombia**, press ↓, type **Dominican Republic**, press ↓, type **Jamaica**, press ↓, type **Mexico**, press ↓, type **Venezuela**, then press ↓

Access places each of the five conditions you specified within quotation marks. Now, you want to set the sort order for the report.

7. Click the **Sort cell** below the Coffee field, click the **Sort list arrow**, then click **Ascending**

Now you're ready to run the updated query.

Time To

√ Save

8. Click the **Run button** on the Query Design toolbar

Figure P1-7 shows the results of the revised query. Now that you have the updated query, you are ready to prepare the custom report.

FIGURE P1-6: **Query results that include data from the Unblended Coffees and Ratings tables**

Fields from the Unblended Coffees table

Field from the Ratings table

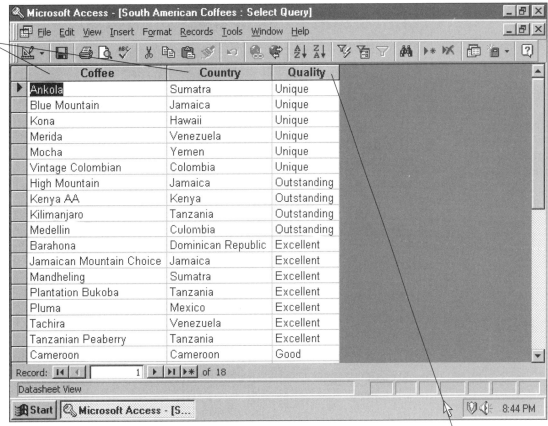

FIGURE P1-7: **Coffees from the Caribbean or South America**

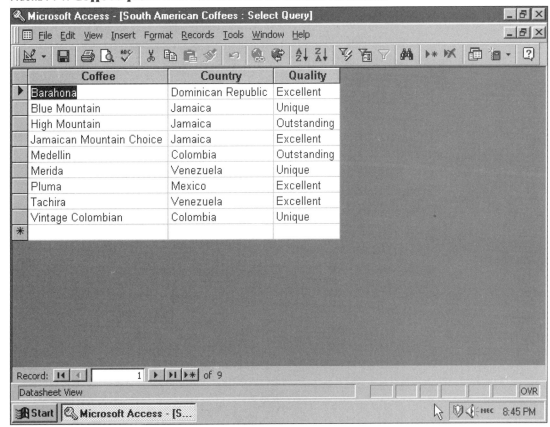

activity:

Prepare and Print a Custom Report

Now that you have updated the query and selected information only on South American coffees, you are ready to produce the custom report for Melanie.

Access 7 Users

If you are using Access 7, click the **New Object** button list arrow , click **New Report**, click **Report Wizard**, then click **OK**.

steps:

1. Click the **New Object button list arrow** on the Query Datasheet toolbar, click **Report**, then double-click **Report Wizard**

   Access shows the name of the current query, "Query: South American Coffees," in the Tables/Queries list box. You want to add all of these fields to your report.

2. Click the **Select All Fields button**, then click **Next**

   The next Report Wizard dialog box asks you how you want to view your data. Access automatically selects "by Unblended Coffees," which is the criterion you want. This option lists the three fields that you want to include in your report. (If you chose "by Ratings," then Access would group coffees by Quality.)

3. Click **Next**, and when Access asks about more grouping levels, click **Next** because you don't want to add any more group levels; then when prompted as to how you want to sort the report data, click the **1 list arrow**, click **Coffee**, then click **Next**

   You want to design the report in a tabular layout, with a Portrait orientation, all fields on one page, and a Soft Gray style.

4. If necessary, click the **Tabular option button** in the Layout area, **Portrait** in the Orientation area, and the **Adjust the field width so all fields fit on a page check box** to select it, then click **Next**, click **Soft Gray** when prompted for the style, then click **Next**

   You want to name the report "South American Coffees".

5. Type **South American Coffees** in the report name box, click the **Preview the report option button** (if necessary), then click **Finish**

   As you examine the finished report, you decide to improve the appearance of the report by adjusting the position and width of the label and text boxes for each of the three fields, starting with the Quality field.

6. Click **Close** on the Print Preview toolbar, then adjust the view so that you can see the Quality label and text boxes, press and hold **[Shift]** while you click the **Quality label box** and the **Quality text box**, release **[Shift]**, position the pointer on the handle on the left side of the Quality text box and when the pointer changes to a double-headed arrow ↔, drag to the right to narrow the width of the **label** and **text boxes**, release the mouse, then, using the same techniques, select and narrow the width of the **Country label box** and the **Country text box**, and select and widen the **Coffee text box**

   Preview, then print your modified report.

Hint

If you need to make further changes to your report layout, switch back to Report Design View, make those changes, then preview and print your report.

7. Preview the report

   Figure P1-8 shows a preview of the custom report at a magnification of 75%. Now you can save the report and close your table.

8. Print and then close the South American Coffees report, query, and the Exotic Imports database

FIGURE P1-8: **Preview of the South American Coffees report**

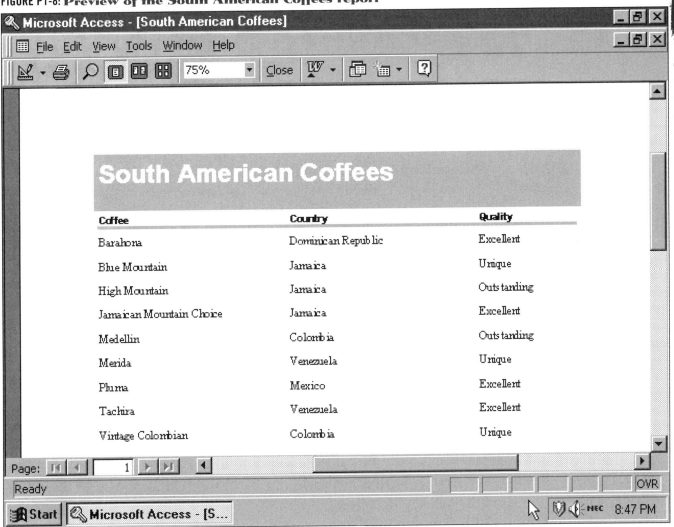

Maintenance Schedule for Hammer Industries Equipment

Hammer Industries, a large commercial builder, maintains a large inventory of vehicles and equipment. The high rate of repairs performed on the company's heavy construction vehicles has been identified as a major expense. Most of these repairs could have been avoided had the company performed routine preventative maintenance on this equipment. Tom Hammer, one of the firm's senior partners, has asked you to help track and forecast the routine equipment maintenance. To develop an equipment maintenance schedule for Hammer Industries, you will **create a database with two related tables**, **create a query that contains a database function** to calculate the next scheduled preventative maintenance (PM) date for each piece of equipment, and **define a custom report** to list the results sorted by ascending maintenance schedule dates.

activity:

Create a Database with Two Related Tables

Using the Table Wizard, you will create an Equipment Master table and a PM History that will contain a description of the equipment, the date it was last serviced, and the number of days between maintenance (DBM).

steps:

1. Start a new database and call it **Hammer Industries**

2. From in the Tables tab click **New**, click **Table Wizard**, then click **OK**

3. Click the **Business option button**, if necessary, then click **Products** in the Sample Tables list

4. Double-click **ProductID**, rename the field **Equipment ID**, double-click **ProductDescription**, rename the field **Description**, double-click **LeadTime**, rename the field **DBM**, then click **Next**

5. Name the table **Equipment Master**, click **Next**, click **Finish**, then enter the data shown in Figure P2-1
Your table should match the one shown in Figure P2-1.

Hint

You can use the AutoNumber feature to assist you when entering key fields.

6. Click the **New Object button list arrow**  on the Table Datasheet toolbar, click **Table**, double-click **Table Wizard**, click **Service Records** from Sample Tables, add the **ServiceRecordID** field to your table and rename it **Maint ID**, add **AssetID** and rename it **Equipment ID**, add **DatePromised** and rename it **Last Maintenance**, add **LaborHours** and rename it **Last Labor Hours**, name the table **PM History**, then finish creating the table

Time To
✓ Save

7. Enter the data shown in Figure P2-2
Your table should match the one shown in Figure P2-2.

FIGURE P2-1: **Equipment Master records 1 to 10**

Microsoft Access - [Equipment Master : Table]

File Edit View Insert Format Records Tools Window Help

Equipment ID	Description	DBM
1	Loader #1	90
2	Grader #3	60
3	Loader #2	90
4	Water Truck #1	120
5	Dump Truck #2	120
6	Grader #4	60
7	Dozer #2	30
8	Dozer #3	30
9	Dump Truck #4	120
10	Dozer #4	30
(AutoNumber)		0

FIGURE P2-2: **PM History records 1 to 10**

Microsoft Access - [PM History : Table]

File Edit View Insert Format Records Tools Window Help

Maint ID	Equipment ID	Last Maintenance	Last Labor Hours
1	3	12/10/98	12
2	1	11/1/97	11
3	2	3/28/98	8
4	5	6/6/98	14
5	9	12/24/97	12
6	6	10/30/97	10
7	10	2/12/98	20
8	4	1/1/98	16
9	8	11/27/97	19
10	7	5/21/98	17
oNumber)			

activity:

Create a Query that Contains a Database Function

Tom would like you to prepare a report that lists a schedule of upcoming maintenance on Hammer Industries equipment. He wants the report to include the Equipment ID number, a description of the equipment, the last date it was serviced, the next scheduled maintenance date (based on the number of days between maintenance), and the number of hours the last maintenance required. To produce this report, you will need to create a query that includes data from both tables and that calculates the next scheduled PM date for each piece of equipment.

Access 7 Users

If you are using Access 7, click New Query after you click the New Object button list arrow .

steps:

1. Click the **New Object button list arrow** [icon] on the Table Datasheet toolbar, click **Query**, then double-click **Simple Query Wizard**
From the Simple Query Wizard, you will need to select the first table and the fields from it that you would like to include in your query.

2. In the Tables/Queries list, click **Table: Equipment Master**, then click the **Select All Fields button** [>>]
You can now add the remaining fields from the other table to the Selected Fields list box.

3. In the Tables/Queries list, click **Table: PM History**, add the fields **Last Maintenance** and **Last Labor Hours** to the Selected Fields list box, click **Next**, then click **Next** again
You can now name your query.

4. Name the query **Hammer PM Schedule**, click the **Open the query to view information option button** (if necessary), click **Finish**, then sort the query in **ascending order** by **Last Maintenance** date
Access shows the requested fields. Your table should match the one shown in Figure P2-3. Now you need to modify the table to include a field that calculates the next scheduled PM date.

Hint

You can maximize the Design View window to see the whole grid.

5. Click the **View button** [icon] on the Query Datasheet toolbar, click the **Show check box** under the DBM field name to deselect it, click the **Last Labor Hours** field name, click **Insert** from the menu bar, click **Columns**, type **Next Maintenance:DateAdd("d",[DBM],[Last Maintenance])**, press ↓ twice, click the **Sort list arrow**, click **Ascending**, then click the **Run button** [icon] on the Query Design toolbar
Your table should match the one shown in Figure P2-4.

6. Save the query

FIGURE P2-3: **Query results**

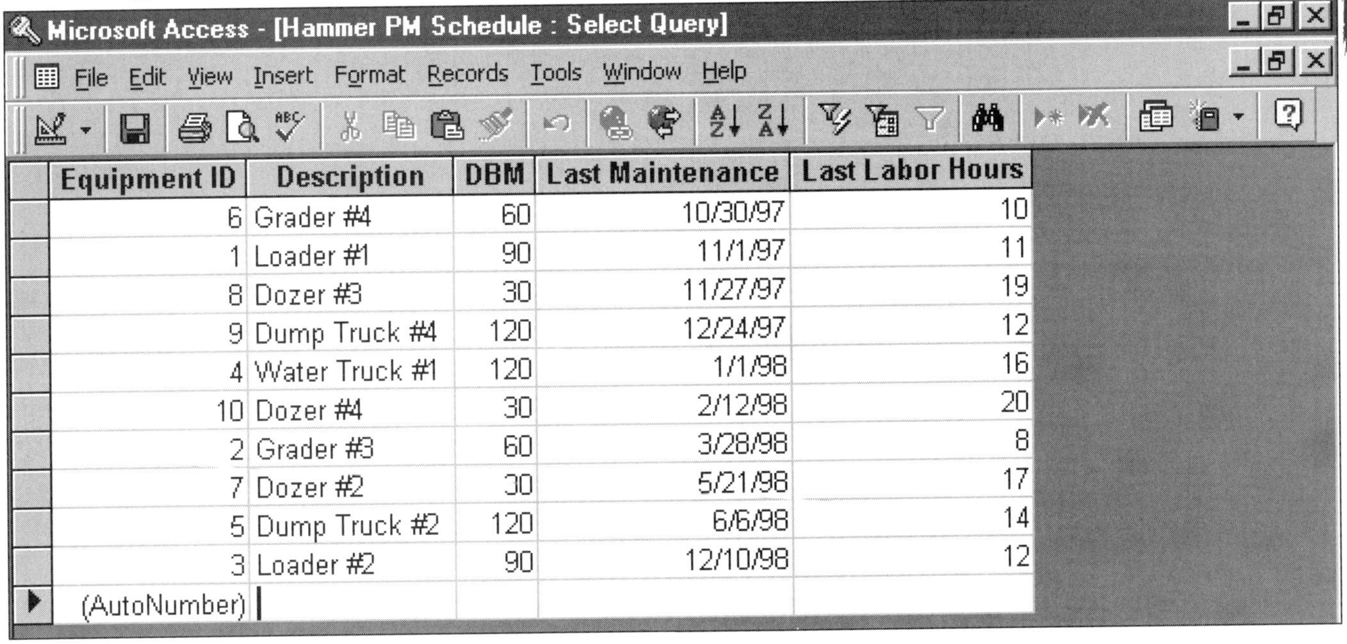

Equipment ID	Description	DBM	Last Maintenance	Last Labor Hours
6	Grader #4	60	10/30/97	10
1	Loader #1	90	11/1/97	11
8	Dozer #3	30	11/27/97	19
9	Dump Truck #4	120	12/24/97	12
4	Water Truck #1	120	1/1/98	16
10	Dozer #4	30	2/12/98	20
2	Grader #3	60	3/28/98	8
7	Dozer #2	30	5/21/98	17
5	Dump Truck #2	120	6/6/98	14
3	Loader #2	90	12/10/98	12
(AutoNumber)				

You can resize column widths to display full field names

FIGURE P2-4: **Modified query results**

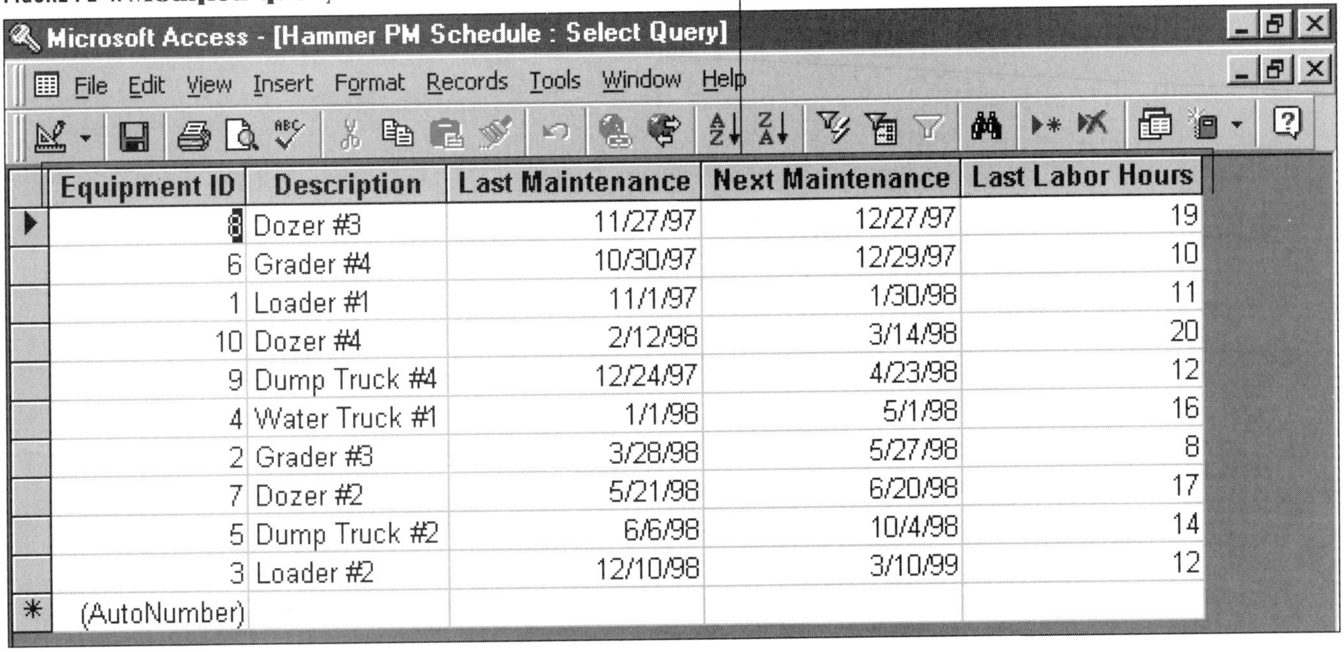

Equipment ID	Description	Last Maintenance	Next Maintenance	Last Labor Hours
8	Dozer #3	11/27/97	12/27/97	19
6	Grader #4	10/30/97	12/29/97	10
1	Loader #1	11/1/97	1/30/98	11
10	Dozer #4	2/12/98	3/14/98	20
9	Dump Truck #4	12/24/97	4/23/98	12
4	Water Truck #1	1/1/98	5/1/98	16
2	Grader #3	3/28/98	5/27/98	8
7	Dozer #2	5/21/98	6/20/98	17
5	Dump Truck #2	6/6/98	10/4/98	14
3	Loader #2	12/10/98	3/10/99	12
(AutoNumber)				

activity:

Define a Custom Report

With the completion of the query definition, you now can define the report. You will use Report Wizard to define a basic report and then modify that report into its final format using Design View.

Access 7 Users

If you are using Access 7, click New Report after you click the New Object button list arrow.

steps:

1. Click the **New Object button list arrow** on the Query Datasheet toolbar, click **Report**, then double-click **Report Wizard**

2. Click the **Select All Fields button** , click **Next**, then when asked about adding any grouping levels, click **Next** again

3. When asked what sort order you want for your records, click the **1 list arrow**, click **Next Maintenance**, then click **Next**

4. Accept the default layout choices for the report (Tabular, Portrait Orientation, and Adjust the field width so all fields fit on a page check box), then click **Next**

5. Click **Corporate** when prompted for the style, then click **Next**

6. Click the **Preview the report option button** (if necessary), click **Finish**, then examine the finished report in the Print Preview window

Hint

You can increase the preview area by changing the Zoom to 75%.

7. Click the **Design View button** on the Print Preview toolbar, modify the report layout so that the final report closely resembles the preview shown in Figure P2-5, and then print it
   You may need to switch between Design view and Print Preview several times to check your results as you modify the layout.

8. Save any modifications to your report as you close the report, the query, and the database

FIGURE P2-5: **Print Preview of Hammer's Maintenance Schedule Report**

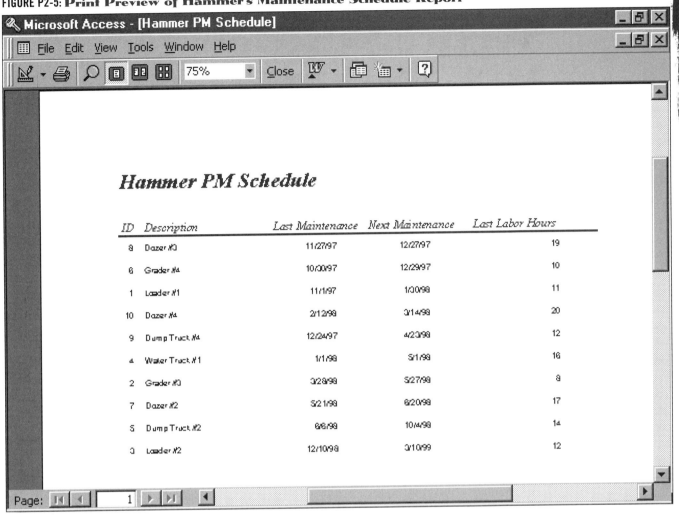

Service Schedule for McNeil's Auto Detail

Toni McNeil owns and operates an auto detailing company. As one of her services, customers can purchase an annual detailing membership that provides them with a weekly detail cleaning of their vehicle. The basic plan provides for a standard interior detailing; however, customers may also subscribe to up to five additional services. Toni would like you to help her maintain a list of her customers and which services they have opted for. She also would like to print a service schedule report sorted by the customer's last name that shows which customers have subscribed to which services. To accomplish these tasks you will **create and query a database** and then **design a custom report** to print the results.

activity:

Create and Query a Database, Design a Custom Report

steps:

Hint

To designate a field as the table key, select the desired field then click the Primary Key button 🔑 on the Table Datasheet toolbar.

1. Create a database named **McNeil Auto Detail**, then use **Design View** to create a table named **Weekly Subscribers**

   Now that the database and table have been created, you can define the fields that will hold the data.

2. Using Design View, define the fields as shown in Figure P3-1, then define the field named **ID** as the table key

   Having defined the fields, you can now enter data.

3. Enter the data as shown in Figure P3-2, adjusting the column widths as needed to accommodate the longest entry in each field, then save the table

   With the data now entered into the Weekly Subscribers table, you can now sort the table.

4. Sort the table in ascending order by last name

   Having sorted the table, you are ready to create Toni's report.

5. Use the Report Wizard to create a custom report that includes all the table fields except ID; when asked about adding and grouping levels, click **Next**; then, when asked what sort order you want for your records, click **Next** again

6. Accept the default layout choices for the report (Tabular, Portrait Orientation, and Adjust the field width so all fields fit on a page check box), click **Next**, click **Corporate** when prompted for the style, then click **Next**

Hint

You will need to use Design View to make sure the First Name field is the first column in the report.

7. Name the report **McNeil's Weekly Subscribers**, click the **Preview the report option button** (if necessary), then click **Finish**

8. Preview the report, and adjust the column widths as necessary to match the report shown in Figure P3-3

   Your report should resemble the one shown in Figure P3-3.

9. Print the report, then save and close the table and the database

FIGURE P3-1: Weekly Subscribers table Design View

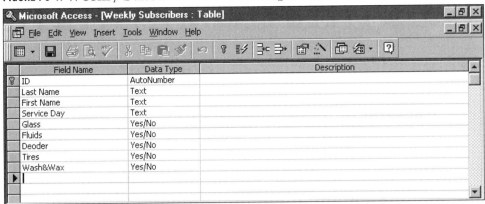

FIGURE P3-2: Data records 1 to 15

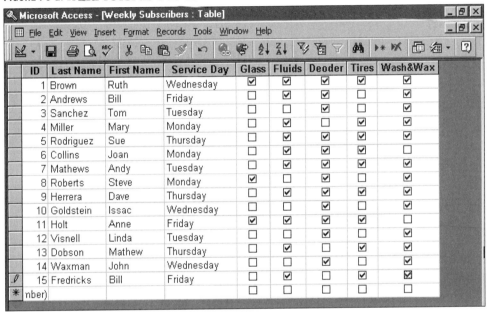

FIGURE P3-3: McNeil's Service Schedule

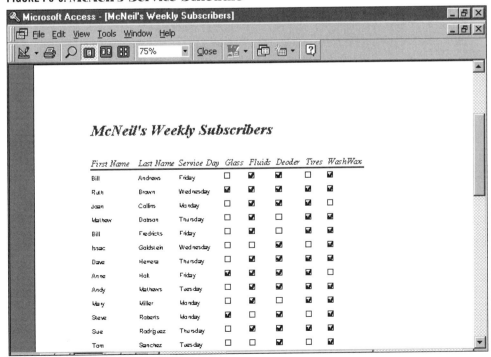

Independent Challenges

INDEPENDENT CHALLENGE 1

You are the owner of Northwest Adventures, Inc., a small mail order business that specializes in canoeing, hiking, and camping equipment. In order to analyze your inventory needs, you decide to build a relational database of products and suppliers, then prepare a report that lists those products and their costs by supplier.

1. Use the worksheet below to plan your database.

Tables	Fields	Primary key

2. Create a database called "Northwest Adventures", then create a table named "Products" that contains the fields listed in the worksheet above and the information shown in Figure IC1-1.

FIGURE IC1-1: Data for records 1 to 18 in the Products table

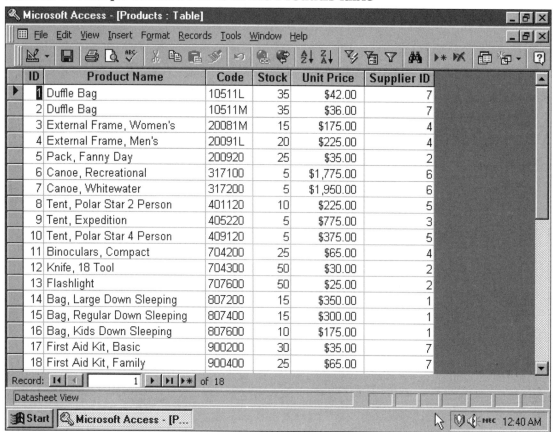

ID	Product Name	Code	Stock	Unit Price	Supplier ID
1	Duffle Bag	10511L	35	$42.00	7
2	Duffle Bag	10511M	35	$36.00	7
3	External Frame, Women's	20081M	15	$175.00	4
4	External Frame, Men's	20091L	20	$225.00	4
5	Pack, Fanny Day	200920	25	$35.00	2
6	Canoe, Recreational	317100	5	$1,775.00	6
7	Canoe, Whitewater	317200	5	$1,950.00	6
8	Tent, Polar Star 2 Person	401120	10	$225.00	5
9	Tent, Expedition	405220	5	$775.00	3
10	Tent, Polar Star 4 Person	409120	5	$375.00	5
11	Binoculars, Compact	704200	25	$65.00	4
12	Knife, 18 Tool	704300	50	$30.00	2
13	Flashlight	707600	50	$25.00	2
14	Bag, Large Down Sleeping	807200	15	$350.00	1
15	Bag, Regular Down Sleeping	807400	15	$300.00	1
16	Bag, Kids Down Sleeping	807600	10	$175.00	1
17	First Aid Kit, Basic	900200	30	$35.00	7
18	First Aid Kit, Family	900400	25	$65.00	7

3. Create a table named "Suppliers" that contains the fields listed in the worksheet above and is related to the Products table in a one-to-many relationship, where one record in the Suppliers table matches many records in the Products table. Complete the table by entering the information shown in Figure IC1-2.

FIGURE IC1-2: Data for records 1 to 7 of the Suppliers table

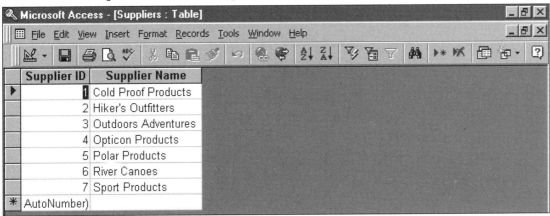

4. Create and run a query that includes the code and product name fields from the Products table, the supplier name field from the Suppliers table, and the unit price field from the Products table. The query should show detail and include all products from Hiker's Outfitters, Opticon Products, and Sport Products.
5. Create an attractively formatted report called "Products by Supplier" that includes all the query fields, shows the data by Suppliers, does not include any additional groupings, and is sorted in ascending order first by product name, then by product code. Preview the report and make any necessary modifications to ensure that all labels and fields are displayed clearly. Then print one copy of the report.

INDEPENDENT CHALLENGE 2

You are head of the Physical Plant at MacKenzie Community College, which, like all other state colleges, receives grants of monies from the state. The governor and state legislative recently adopted a plan that calls for a very gradual reduction in monies for colleges over the next five years. To prepare for the reduced funding for service and maintenance, you decide to build a relational database that tracks service and maintenance costs for different departments within the college. You then can use the database to project and analyze costs.

1. Use the worksheet below to plan your database.

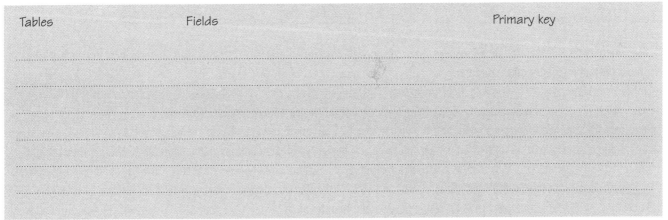

2. Create a database called "MacKenzie Community College", then create a table called "Service and Maintenance Expenses" that contains the fields listed in the worksheet above and the information shown in Figure IC2-1.

FIGURE IC2-1: Data for records 1 to 15 in the Service and Maintenance Expenses table

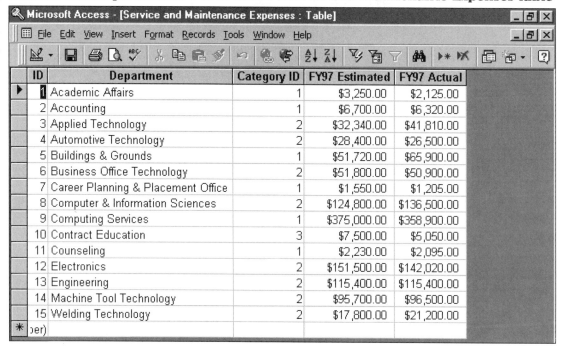

3. Create a table named "Expense Categories" that contains the fields listed in the worksheet above and that is related to the Service and Maintenance Expenses table in a one-to-many relationship, where one record matches many records in the Service and Maintenance Expenses table. Complete the table using the data shown in Figure IC2-2.

FIGURE IC2-2: Data for records 1 to 3 of the Expense Categories table

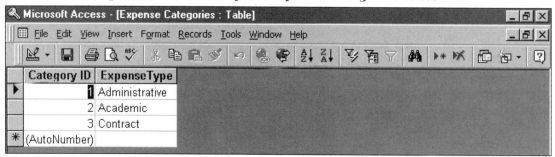

4. Filter the Service and Maintenance Expenses table to show all departments with a Category ID of 1, then print one copy of the filtered database, then remove the filter.
5. Create an advanced filter to show all departments with a Category ID of 1 or 3, print the results, then remove the filter.
6. Create a select query that includes the Department field from the Service and Maintenance Expenses table, the expense type field from the Expense Categories table, and the Fiscal Year 97 Estimated and Fiscal Year 97 Actual fields from the Service and Maintenance Expenses table (in that order). Modify the query design so that it contains two calculated fields: a Variance field and an FY98 Projected field. Calculate the Variance by finding the difference between Fiscal Year 97 Actual and Fiscal Year 97 Estimated. Calculate the FY98 Projected field by adding 15% of the Variance to the Fiscal Year 97 Actual field.
7. Create and print a report called "1998 Projected Service and Maintenance Costs" that shows the results of your modified query. The report should list the data by expense categories, and the expense types should be sorted in ascending order by department.

INDEPENDENT CHALLENGE 3

Create a personal phone list that contains information about your personal and business associates. For example, you might include such data as the person's first and last name; their street address, city, state and zip; their professional title; their company and its street address, city, state and zip; their home phone, modem, and fax numbers; and their business phone, modem, and fax numbers.

1. Create a database called "Phone List", then create a table called "Personal and Business Contacts". Enter data for 12 to 15 people, making sure to include both personal friends and business contacts.
2. Sort the list by Last Name.
3. Change the table's design by inserting a new text field named "Personal/Business".
4. Update the records by entering a "P" or a "B" in the Personal/Business field to indicate whether each contact in your phone list is Personal or Business related.
5. Use a filter to list only the Personal records; then create another filter to list only the Business records. After creating each filter, design and print a custom report showing the filtered data.

INDEPENDENT CHALLENGE 4

As an organic grocer, you pride yourself on growing and selling the region's best organic produce. Over the years you have gathered planting information about those vegetables that sell the best, and you would like to organize this data in a useful manner so that you can access it quickly and easily.

1. Create a database called Garden, then create a table called Vegetables. Complete the table by entering the data shown in Figure IC4-1.
2. Sort and print the list in ascending order by Vegetable name.
3. Sort and print the list in ascending order by Time to plant.
4. Sort and print the list in ascending order of Maturity.
5. Filter your data to list only those vegetables planted in Mid Spring.
6. Use the Report Wizard to create an attractive, easy-to-read report of the filtered data.

FIGURE IC4-1: **Vegetable data**

Vegetable	Hardiness	Time to plant	Soil pH	Maturity
Potatoes, Sweet	Sensitive	Mid Spring	5.5	60 days
Beans, Snap	Very Sensitive	Early Spring	6.8	60 days
Cucumbers	Sensitive	Late Spring	7	70 days
Broccoli	Hardy	Early Spring	6.5	80 days
Cauliflower	Hardy	Mid Spring	6.5	90 days
Carrots	Hardy	Mid Spring	6	70 days
Corn, Sweet	Sensitive	Early Spring	6.5	85 days
Cabbage	Hardy	Early Spring	6.5	110 days
Lettuce	Hardy	Early Spring	6.5	80 days
Onions	Hardy	Early Spring	6	120 days
Beets	Very Hardy	Early Spring	6.5	55 days
Tomatoes	Sensitive	Mid Spring	4	110 days
Squash	Sensitive	Early Spring	6.5	55 days
Beans, Lima	Very Sensitive	Mid Spring	6	90 days

Visual Workshop

Create a table called "Item Master", as shown in Figure VW-1. After completing this table, create the custom report shown in Figure VW-2.

FIGURE VW-1: Item Master table

	Item #	Description	Retail	Vendor	Shelf	Bin	Qty On Hand	Qty On Order
	776	Drive, 1.2Gb	$225.95	Maxtor	5	3	4	6
	879	Drive, Zip	$199.95	Iomega	3	2	4	4
	907	CD, 4x	$59.95	Panasonic	22	7	8	4
	982	CD, 8x	$79.95	Mitsumi	22	5B	5	4
	983	Thinkpad 365XD	$2,450.00	IBM	2	2	2	2
	3001	Cable, Parallel, 12'	$4.95	Western	12	3A	15	12
	4948	Monitor, 17"	$785.00	Mitsubichi	19	1	4	0
	8383	Cable, Parallel, 15'	$5.00	J&P	12	3B	10	12
	9373	Multimedia Kit, 4x	$325.95	Creative Labs	19	2	6	0
	40221	Prolinea 575e	$1,895.00	Compaq	6	1	5	0
	83745	Cable, Serial 25'	$5.75	Western	12	6B	16	0

FIGURE VW-2: Item Master report

Microsoft
► Access
Projects

Client and Customer Databases

In This Unit You Will Create A:

► **Mailing List**

► **Client list**

► **Phone List**

By using a relational database program such as Access, you can track important information for a company or business—such as a client list, customer list, supplier list, inventory list, price list, etc.—and then work with one or more tables to create custom queries and reports that produce the information you need. If you work as an employee or volunteer in a membership or non-profit organization, you can track such information as members and their interests, donors, media contacts, the voting records of politicians, and policy issues. In each case, you can quickly and easily produce custom reports and mailing labels. ► In this unit you will learn how to use Microsoft Access to create and work with client and customer databases. You will create relational and non-relational database tables with the Table Wizard and Design View, design forms, enter data in a form, create queries with calculated fields, create custom reports, and produce mailing labels.

Mailing List for Prescott Symphony Subscribers

Daniel Genzler, the new administrative director of the Prescott Symphony, has ambitious plans for increasing the Symphony's subscriber base. He wants you to create a subscriber list. Since this list comprises approximately 2,400 suppliers, you decide to create a custom form to simplify the data entry process. Daniel also wants you to include the Series in which each subscriber enrolled and indicate whether the subscriber is a Friend of the Symphony. The Symphony will use this subscriber list to mail brochures of the upcoming season's events, to promote membership in their Friend of the Symphony program, and to track individual interests and contributions.

Project Activities

Create the Subscriber Database

Because the Symphony's subscriber mailing list is similar to other types of client and customer databases used by businesses, you decide to use the Table Wizard to create the database table from the Contacts Sample table. Then, you can define the additional fields you need for this specific table of Series subscribers.

Create a Data Entry Form

To simplify the data entry process, you will use the Form Wizard to create a custom form. Later, the Symphony can hire interns or temporary employees to assist with the data entry for the 2,400 subscribers plus any new enrollments. The form will make it easier for interns and temporary employees to enter the data.

Create a Series Report

Daniel wants you to print a report that includes the names of subscribers organized by the Series in which each enrolled. You will use the Report Wizard to build the custom report.

Create Mailing Labels

Daniel also wants you to print mailing labels so that he and his staff can send a brochure describing a special event that the Symphony has added to this season's performances. To save money on the mailing, he asks that you print the mailing labels in zip code and street address order. You will use the Label Wizard to produce the labels.

When you have completed Project 1, the custom report will appear as shown in Figure P1-1.

FIGURE P1-1: **Prescott Symphony Subscribers**

Prescott Symphony Subscribers

Series	Last Name	First Name	Title	Friend
A				
	Lee	David	Mr.	☐
	Morgan	Christopher	Mr.	☑
	Snowden	Helen	Ms.	☐
B				
	Landen	Richard	Mr.	☐
	Shoupe	Jim	Mr.	☐
C				
	Herrera	Jose	Mr.	☐
	Howard	Karen	Ms.	☑
	Martin	Melinda	Ms.	☑
D				
	Kardish	Adella	Ms.	☑
F				
	Britton	Debbie	Ms.	☐
	Grove	Sharon	Ms.	☑
	Mathias	Lloyd	Mr.	☑
G				
	Jones	Sarah	Ms.	☑
	Pierce	Lilian	Ms.	☐
	Wieser	Michael	Mr.	☑

Clues to Use

In real life, client and customer databases might easily contain thousands or millions of records. When you work with one of those databases, you perform the same types of operations that you perform in this project; however, you just enter and process more data.

activity:

Create the Subscriber Database

After examining the paper records the Symphony keeps on its program subscribers and after discussing with Daniel the potential uses of this new database, you decide to include fields for the customer ID, title, first name, last name, two address lines, city, state, zip code, series enrollment, and Friend of the Symphony.

steps:

1. Start Microsoft Access, then create a database named **Prescott Symphony Subscribers** on the data disk where you are saving your files for this book

Because the Prescott Symphony Subscribers database will be similar to client and customer contact lists used by other businesses and organizations, you can use the Table Wizard to define the database.

2. On the Tables sheet of the Prescott Symphony Subscribers: Database window, click **New**, double-click **Table Wizard** in the New Table dialog box, then click **Contacts** in the Sample Tables list

You need the customer ID, title, first name, last name, address, city, state, and zip fields.

3. Double-click **ContactID** in the Sample Fields list box and rename it **ID**, double-click **Title**, double-click **FirstName**, double-click **LastName**, double-click **Address** and rename it **Address1**, double-click **Address** and rename it **Address2**, double-click **City**, double-click **StateOrProvince** and rename it **State**, double-click **PostalCode** and rename it **Zip**, then click **Next**

Now you can name the table, set the primary key, and switch to Design View so you can add two new fields.

4. Type **Subscribers** in the table name box, click the **Yes, set a primary key for me option button** (if necessary), click **Next**, click the **Modify the table design option button**, then click **Finish**

The Series field that you want to add will contain a one- or two-letter code to identify different Symphony series. The Friend field will indicate whether or not the subscriber is a Friend of the Symphony.

5. Maximize the Design View window, click in the next available cell in the Field Name column, type **Series**, press **[Enter]**, double-click the **default setting of 50** in the Field Size property box, then type **2**, click in the next available cell in the Field Name column, type **Friend**, click the **Data Type list arrow** for the Friend field, then click **Yes/No**

You decide to change the sizes of the Address1 and Address2 fields to conserve space on the form.

Trouble?

Depending on your screen resolution, you might not be able to see the first two fields: the ID field with the AutoNumber data type and the Title field with the Text data type.

6. Click the **Data Type cell** for the Address1 field, double-click **Field Size setting of 255**, type **50**, click the **Data Type cell** for the Address2 field, double-click **Field Size setting of 255**, then type **50**

Check your field definitions against those shown in Figure P1-2.

7. Click the **View button** ▦▾ on the Table Design toolbar

8. Click **OK** to save your changes to the table design

FIG P1-2: Field definitions for the Subscribers table

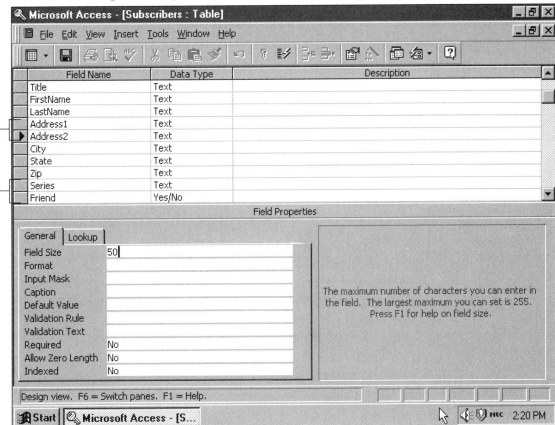

Adjust the Field Sizes of the Address1 and Address2 fields

Add the Series and Friend fields and define their data types

activity:

Create a Data Entry Form

To simplify the data entry for the interns and temporary employees who will work on this database, you want to use the Form Wizard to create a custom form with an interesting background. Furthermore, you want to include all the fields on one screen so that you can view all the data on each subscriber.

Access 7 Users

If you are using Access 7.0, click the **New Object button list arrow**, click **New Form**, click **Form Wizard**, then click **OK**.

steps:

1. Click the **New Object button list arrow** on the Table Datasheet toolbar, click **Form**, then double-click **Form Wizard**

   You want to include all the fields in your new table in the custom form.

2. Click the **Add All Fields button**, then click **Next**

   You decide to use the Columnar layout for the form and, from your previous examination of the styles, you decide the Dusk style would be the most appropriate style for the Prescott Symphony.

3. Click the **Columnar option button** (if necessary), click **Next**, click **Dusk** in the list of available styles, then click **Next**

   You decide to accept the default name for the form. Also, you want to view the form before making any changes.

4. Click the **Open the form to view or enter information option button** (if necessary), then click **Finish**

   Access shows the form created with the Form Wizard. You decide to add a title to identify the form's purpose.

5. Click the **View button** on the Form View toolbar, position the mouse pointer between the Form Header and Detail sections and when the pointer changes to ✛, drag the Detail section down to the ½-inch mark on the left ruler; if you do not see a Toolbox toolbar, click **View** on the menu bar, then click **Toolbox**

   Now you can add a label box to the Form Header section.

Hint

You might need to move the label box and position it where you want the title to appear.

6. Click the **Label button** **Aa** on the Toolbox toolbar, click in the upper-left corner of the Form Header section, type **Prescott Symphony Subscribers** in the label box, then click the **Form Header bar**

   So that the title appears more prominent on the form, you decide to increase its font size.

7. Click the **Prescott Symphony Subscribers label box**, click the **Font Size list arrow** on the Formatting (Form/Report) toolbar, click **24**, drag one or more of the sizing handles to resize the label box so that all text displays clearly, then close the Toolbox toolbar

   Now you can view your modified form and begin entering subscribers in the database table.

Hint

To add a check mark to the Friend field to indicate a subscriber is a Friend of the Symphony, click the check box or press the [Spacebar].

8. Click the **View button** on the Form Design toolbar to switch to Form View, as shown in Figure P1-3, then use the form to enter the data shown in Figure P1-4

9. After entering the data, save and close the table

FIGURE P1-3: **Prescott Symphony Subscribers form**

Form View for entering data

Title for custom form

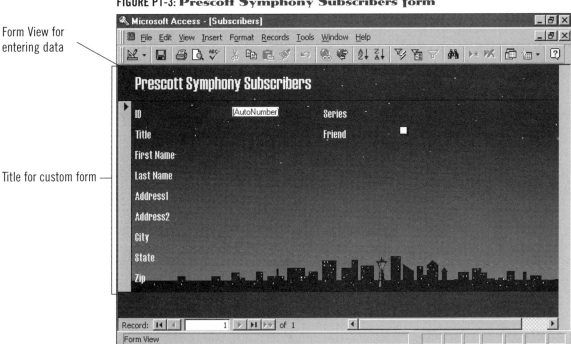

FIGURE P1-4: **Data for records 1 to 15 of the Prescott Symphony Subscribers table**

Series Enrollee	Series	Friend	Series Enrollee	Series	Friend
Ms. Sarah Jones 5298 Hall Road Prescott, CA 95436-0212	G	Yes	Ms. Debbie Britton 1551 Valencia Street Apartment #5 San Rafael, CA 94903-2387	F	No
Mr. Richard Landen 45 Ravenwood Court Apartment #1 Prescott, CA 95436-0212	B	No	Ms. Melinda Martin 506 Avalon Way Sonoma, CA 95426-0265	C	Yes
Ms. Helen Snowden 2530 Chapman Way Forestville, CA 95436-0212	A	No	Ms. Lilian Pierce 1182 Wood Road Prescott, CA 95436-0212	G	No
Mr. Michael Wieser 1447 Kerry Lane Redwood City, CA 94063-0531	G	Yes	Mr. Lloyd Mathias 136 Brookview Court Apartment #7 Scotts Valley, CA 95066-4354	F	Yes
Ms. Karen Howard 1605 Henning Street Walnut Creek, CA 94956-8391	C	Yes	Mr. Jose Herrera 525 Gayle Road Prescott, CA 95436-0212	C	No
Mr. Jim Shoupe 5168 Mountain Road Fresno, CA 93727-2231	B	No	Ms. Adella Kardish 1346 Alan Way Prescott, CA 95436-0212	D	Yes
Mr. Christopher Morgan 1851 Salem Way Prescott, CA 95436-0212	A	Yes	Mr. David Lee 179 Meadowside Court Forestville, CA 95436-0212	A	No
Ms. Sharon Grove 1000 Shiloh Road S. San Francisco, CA 94083-5959	F	Yes			

activity:

Create a Series Report

Now that you have completed the entry of the first set of Series subscribers in the Symphony's Mailing List database, you want to design and print a report of subscribers by Series. Daniel and his staff can then use the report to discuss and develop strategies for increasing the number of subscribers who contribute to the Symphony as part of the Friends of the Symphony program.

steps:

1. In the Microsoft Access Database window, click the **Reports tab**, click **New**, click **Report Wizard**, and when prompted by the Report Wizard about which fields to include in your report, click the **Tables/Queries list arrow** if you do not see a table name, click **Subscribers**, then click **OK**
You want to include only the Title, FirstName, LastName, Series, and Friend fields in the report.

2. Double-click **Title** in the Available Fields list box, double-click **FirstName**, double-click **LastName**, double-click **Series**, double-click **Friend**, then click **Next**
So that you can tell which Series are the most popular among subscribers, you want to group the subscribers by Series in the report.

3. Double-click **Series** in the Fields list box, then click **Next**
You want to list subscribers in order first by last name, then by first name.

4. Click the **1 list arrow**, click **LastName**, click the **2 list arrow**, click **FirstName**, click **Next**
You decide to use the Stepped layout and the Casual style for the report.

5. In the Layout area, click the **Stepped option button** (if necessary), click **Portrait** in the Orientation area (if necessary), click the **Adjust the field width so all fields fit on a page check** box to select it (if necessary), click **Next**, click **Casual** when prompted for the style, then click **Next**
After naming the report, you want to preview it.

6. Type **Prescott Symphony Subscribers** in the report name box, click the **Preview the report option button** (if necessary), click **Finish**, review the finished report in the Print Preview window, then click **Close** on the Print Preview toolbar

7. Using Figure P1-5 as a guide, adjust the width of the Friend label box
After modifying your report, you want to preview it again, before printing it.

8. Preview and print the report

9. Save and close the report

FIGURE P1-5: Adjusting the width of the Friend label box in Report Design

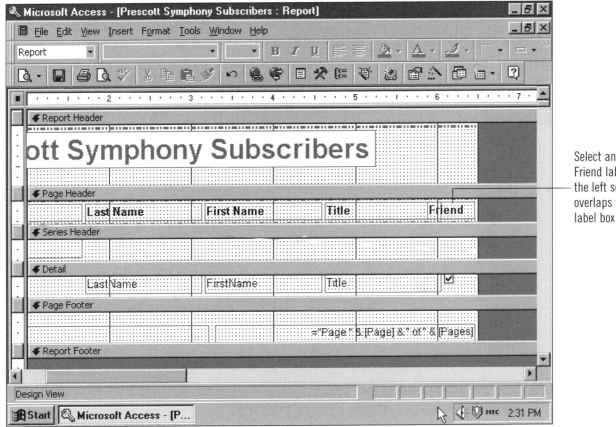

Select and drag the Friend label box to the left so that it overlaps the Title label box

Clues to Use

If you want to improve the alignment of report headings and report detail, you can drag a label or text box so that it overlaps the beginning of a label or text box in another column where nothing will print. You also can widen or narrow fields as desired.

activity:

Create Mailing Labels

Your final task is to print mailing labels that Daniel and his staff will use to send a brochure describing a special event that the Symphony has added to this season's performances. You can use the Label Wizard to simplify this process and to place the labels in zip code order so that the Symphony can use bulk mailing and reduce its postage costs.

steps:

1. In the Microsoft Access Database window, click the **Reports tab**, click **New**, click **Label Wizard**, click **Subscribers** in the table or query name list box, then click **OK**
The mailing labels will need the Title, FirstName, LastName, Address1, Address2, City, State, and Zip fields.

2. When prompted by the Label Wizard about the label size, click **Avery number 5160**, click **Next**, and when prompted for the font and color of the text, click **Next** to use the default font and color
Next, you design the format of the label and include the fields you want to print. The first line on the label will include the Title, FirstName, and LastName fields.

3. Double-click **Title** in the Available fields list box, press **[Spacebar]**, double-click **FirstName**, press **[Spacebar]**, double-click **LastName**, then press **[Enter]**
Now you can complete the address block for the Prototype label.

4. Double-click **Address1** in the Available fields list box, press **[Enter]**, double-click **Address2**, press **[Enter]**, double-click **City**, type **,** (a comma), press **[Spacebar]**, double-click **State**, press **[Spacebar]** twice, then double-click **Zip**
Your Prototype label should be identical to the one shown in Figure P1-6. You want to sort the labels by zip code, city, and street address to save money by bulk mailing.

5. Click **Next** and when prompted for the fields for sorting the labels, double-click **Zip** in the Available fields list box, double-click **City**, double-click **Address1**, click **Next**, and when prompted for the report name, type **Prescott Symphony Mailing List Labels**, click the **See the labels as they will look printed option button** (if necessary), then click **Finish**
Now you can print the mailing labels, if you have the label sheets available.

6. Print the mailing labels
Your sheet of mailing labels should be similar to the one shown in Figure P1-7. If you don't have mailing label sheets, just use a plain sheet of paper.

7. Save and close the report and database

FIGURE P1-6: **Prototype label for the Prescott Symphony mailing list**

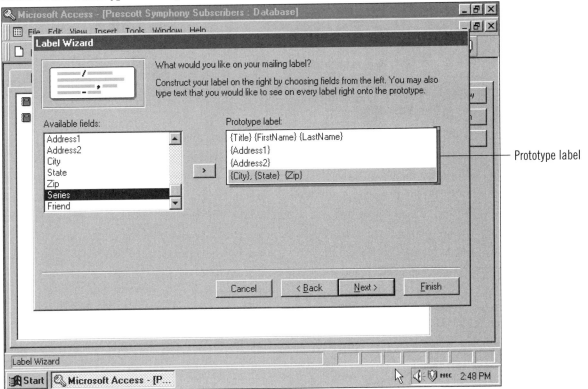

Prototype label

FIGURE P1-7: **Mailing labels for the Prescott Symphony**

Mr. Jim Shoupe
5168 Mountain Road
Fresno, CA 937272231

Mr. Michael Wieser
1447 Kerry Lane
Redwood City, CA 940630531

Ms. Sharon Grove
1000 Shiloh Road
S. San Francisco, CA 940835959

Ms. Debbie Britton
1551 Valencia Street
Apartment #5
San Rafael, CA 949032387

Ms. Karen Howard
1605 Henning Street
Walnut Creek, CA 949568391

Mr. Lloyd Mathias
136 Brookview Court
Apartment #7
Scotts Valley, CA 950664354

Ms. Melinda Martin
506 Avalon Way
Sonoma, CA 954260265

Mr. David Lee
179 Meadowside Court
Forestville, CA 954360212

Ms. Helen Snowden
2530 Chapman Way
Forestville, CA 954360212

Ms. Lilian Pierce
1182 Wood Road
Prescott, CA 954360212

Ms. Adella Kardish
1346 Alan Way
Prescott, CA 954360212

Mr. Christopher Morgan
1851 Salem Way
Prescott, CA 954360212

Mr. Richard Landen
45 Ravenwood Court
Apartment #1
Prescott, CA 954360212

Mr. Jose Herrera
525 Gayle Road
Prescott, CA 954360212

Ms. Sarah Jones
5928 Hall Road
Prescott, CA 954360212

OVERVIEW

Client List for Wilson Investments' Grand Opening

Wilson Investments, a growing investment brokerage firm, plans to expand its operations into a nearby metropolitan area in which it has an existing client base. As marketing manager of Wilson Investments, you would like to invite clients currently living within the new branch's market area that have invested over $250,000 with the firm to a private reception celebrating the grand opening. The market area for the new branch will encompass the geographic area falling under the 55474 zip code. You determine that you can access data from two database tables, the Investment Summary table and the Client Master table, to decide which clients to invite to the opening. You will **design and enter data for two related tables**, create **a query with a calculated field**, and then **create a custom report**.

activity:

Design and Enter Data for Two Related Tables

You will create a database and, using Table Wizard, define two tables. The first table will contain investment data. It will identify clients, and up to three investment plans and corresponding investment amounts. The second table will provide the names and addresses of Wilson Investments' clients.

steps:

Hint

Access categorizes sample tables as either Business or Personal. For this exercise you will need to select the Business radio button to display the sample business tables list.

1. Start **Access**, then create a new database based on the **Blank Database template**, name the database **Wilson Investments** and save it to the disk on which you are saving your files

   First, you'll design and enter the data for the Investment Summary table.

2. Click the **Tables tab**, click **New**, double-click **Table Wizard** in the New Table dialog box, then click **Payments** in the Sample Tables list of the Business category

3. Select the **CustomerID** and rename it **Client ID**, select **ProjectID** and rename it **Invest1 ID**, select **PaymentAmount** and rename it **Invest1 Amt**, select **ProjectID** and rename it **Invest2 ID**, select **PaymentAmount** and rename it **Invest2 Amt**, select **ProjectID** and rename it **Invest3 ID**, select **PaymentAmount** and rename it **Invest3 Amt**, click **Next**, name the table **Investment Summary**, click **Next**, then click **Finish**

   Having defined the Investment Summary table, you now can enter the data for this table.

Hint

When you create more than one table for a single database, Microsoft Access will ask you whether the tables you have created are related (linked). Linked tables must have a duplicate field in both tables. It's a good idea to have only one linking field with the same field name in both tables.

4. Enter the data shown in Figure P2-1 into the Investment Summary table, then close the table

   Your table should resemble the one shown in Figure P2-1. You now are ready to create the second table.

5. Click the **Tables tab**, use **Table Wizard** to create a new table, then click **Customers** in the Sample Tables list

   The Customers sample table contains all the fields you want to use in this table, although you will rename a few of them.

6. Select **CustomerID** and rename it **Client ID**, select **CompanyName** and rename it **Name**, select **BillingAddress** and rename it **Address**, select **City**, select **StateOrProvince** and rename it **State**, select **PostalCode** and rename it **Zip**, click **Next**, name the table **Client Master**, click **Next**, click **Next**, then click **Finish**

   Having defined the Client Master table and specified that it is linked to the Investment Summary table, you now can enter the data for this table.

Time To

✓ Save
✓ Close

7. Enter the data shown in Figure P2-2

   Your table should resemble the one shown in Figure P2-2.

FIGURE P2-1: **Data records 1 through 15 for the Investment Summary table**

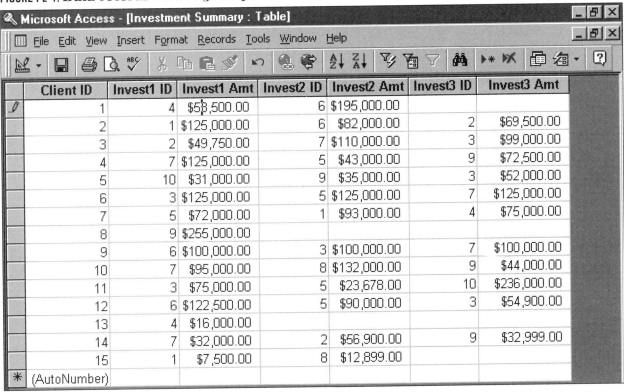

Client ID	Invest1 ID	Invest1 Amt	Invest2 ID	Invest2 Amt	Invest3 ID	Invest3 Amt
1	4	$58,500.00	6	$195,000.00		
2	1	$125,000.00	6	$82,000.00	2	$69,500.00
3	2	$49,750.00	7	$110,000.00	3	$99,000.00
4	7	$125,000.00	5	$43,000.00	9	$72,500.00
5	10	$31,000.00	9	$35,000.00	3	$52,000.00
6	3	$125,000.00	5	$125,000.00	7	$125,000.00
7	5	$72,000.00	1	$93,000.00	4	$75,000.00
8	9	$255,000.00				
9	6	$100,000.00	3	$100,000.00	7	$100,000.00
10	7	$95,000.00	8	$132,000.00	9	$44,000.00
11	3	$75,000.00	5	$23,678.00	10	$236,000.00
12	6	$122,500.00	5	$90,000.00	3	$54,900.00
13	4	$16,000.00				
14	7	$32,000.00	2	$56,900.00	9	$32,999.00
15	1	$7,500.00	8	$12,899.00		
* (AutoNumber)						

FIGURE P2-2: **Data records 1 through 15 for the Client Master table**

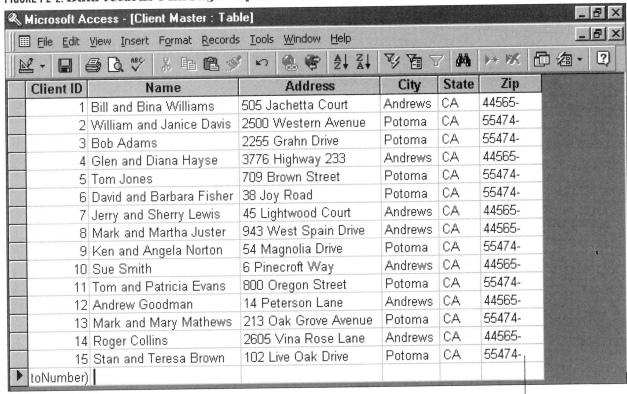

Client ID	Name	Address	City	State	Zip
1	Bill and Bina Williams	505 Jachetta Court	Andrews	CA	44565-
2	William and Janice Davis	2500 Western Avenue	Potoma	CA	55474-
3	Bob Adams	2255 Grahn Drive	Potoma	CA	55474-
4	Glen and Diana Hayse	3776 Highway 233	Andrews	CA	44565-
5	Tom Jones	709 Brown Street	Potoma	CA	55474-
6	David and Barbara Fisher	38 Joy Road	Potoma	CA	55474-
7	Jerry and Sherry Lewis	45 Lightwood Court	Andrews	CA	44565-
8	Mark and Martha Juster	943 West Spain Drive	Andrews	CA	44565-
9	Ken and Angela Norton	54 Magnolia Drive	Potoma	CA	55474-
10	Sue Smith	6 Pinecroft Way	Andrews	CA	44565-
11	Tom and Patricia Evans	800 Oregon Street	Potoma	CA	55474-
12	Andrew Goodman	14 Peterson Lane	Andrews	CA	44565-
13	Mark and Mary Mathews	213 Oak Grove Avenue	Potoma	CA	55474-
14	Roger Collins	2605 Vina Rose Lane	Andrews	CA	44565-
15	Stan and Teresa Brown	102 Live Oak Drive	Potoma	CA	55474-

Access leaves space for extended zip codes

CLIENT LIST FOR WILSON INVESTMENTS' GRAND OPENING

activity:

Create a Query with a Calculated Field

In order to create a list of clients to invite to the reception, you will need to query the Client Master table for all records containing the 55474 zip code and the Investment Summary table for all records whose total investments are equal to or greater than $250,000. Because there is no currently defined field that shows the investment total for each client, you will need to calculate this amount. To accomplish these tasks you will create a simple query and then modify it using Design View.

steps:

1. From the **Queries tab**, create a new query using the **Simple Query Wizard**

You now can define the query for all clients residing within the 55474 area code.

2. Select all the fields from the Client Master table

3. From the Investment Summary table, select **Invest1 Amt**, select **Invest2 Amt**, select **Invest3 Amt**, click **Next**, click **Detail (shows every field of every record)**, click **Next**, name the query **55474 Clients**, click **Modify the query design option button**, then click **Finish**

Not all the fields you have selected need appear on the query. Although you have selected the client's three investment amounts, you have done so in order to calculate and display the client's total investment. You need to tell Microsoft Access which fields you do not want it to show.

4. Deselect the Show check box for **Client ID**, deselect the Show check box for **Invest1 Amt**, deselect the Show check box for **Invest2 Amt**, then deselect the Show check box for **Invest3 Amt**

You now can create a new field to calculate the total investment dollars for each client.

5. Click the **empty cell adjacent to Invest3 Amt**, then type **Total Investment: [Invest1 Amt]+[Invest2 Amt]+[Invest3 Amt]**

Now that you have selected all the fields you need to create the final report, you must enter the criteria that will allow you to report on all clients living within the 55474 zip code who have invested a total of $250,000 or more.

6. Click the first blank Criteria cell under the Zip field, type **55474**, click the first blank Criteria cell under the Total Investment field, then type **>=250000**

Having completed the query definition, you can now run it.

Hint

Depending on the screen resolution of your PC's monitor, you may not be able to see all the fields on your screen.

7. Click the **Run button** 🔘 on the Query Design toolbar

The records that meet the criteria you specified are listed in Query Table View, as shown in Figure P2-4.

8. Save the query

FIGURE P2-3: **Query Design View for 55474 Clients Select Query**

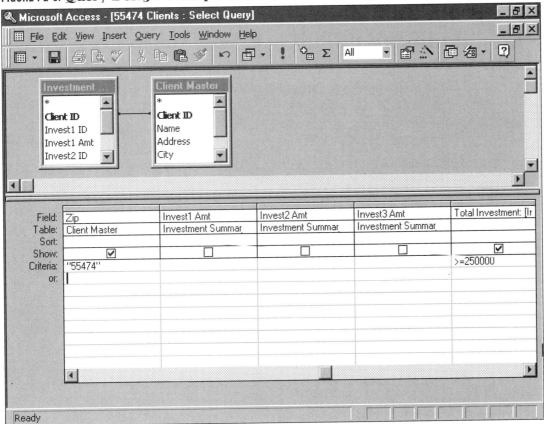

FIGURE P2-4: **Query Table View for 55474 Clients Select Query**

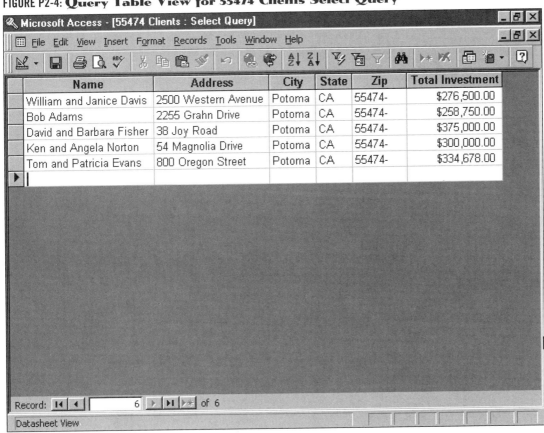

Access 97

activity:

Create a Custom Report

You will use the Report Wizard to create a custom report that contains the clients' names, the total amount of their investments managed by the company, and the clients' addresses.

Access 7 Users

If you are using Access 7, click New Report after clicking the **New Object button list arrow** 組 ▾ .

steps:

1. Click the **New Object button list arrow** 組 ▾ on the Query Datasheet toolbar, then click **Report**

   You must tell the Report Wizard which information to display on the report. Because you have already defined a query of the fields you would like to report on, you can select some or all of these fields for your report.

2. Double-click **Report Wizard**, click the **Select All Fields button** ❯❯ , then click **Next**

   The Report Wizard allows you to define certain fields as group headers, which appear on their own line just before the report detail. You will define the Name and Total Investment fields as group headers so that this information will stand out in the report.

3. Select **Name** and **Total Investment** as group headers

   Having selected the information you would like to emphasize as group headers, you now will select a report format that indents the detail lines for each record under these headers.

4. Select the **Outline 1** format, select the **Soft Gray** style, click the **Preview the report option button** (if necessary), then click **Finish**

   Compare your screen to Figure P2-5.

5. Print your report by clicking on the **Print button** 🖨 on the Print Preview toolbar

6. Click **Close** on the Print Preview toolbar, then save and close the Wilson Investments database

FIGURE P2-5: 55474 Clients Report

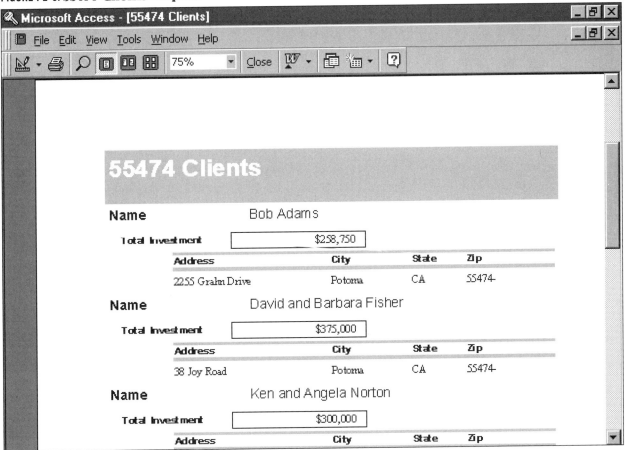

CLIENT AND CUSTOMER DATABASES   AC B-17

Donor Phone List for the Children's Council

You are the director of sponsorship for Children's Council, a nationwide, non-profit, charitable organization. You have been asked by the organization's president, Sue Anderson, to personally finalize donation agreements with the organization's 15 largest donors. As part of your preparation for these visits, you want to put together a listing of these donors' phone and fax numbers, sorted by the donor's last name, so the contact information is readily available. To do so, you will **create a phone list and then format and print the phone list**.

activity:

Create a Phone List

Using the Table Wizard, you will quickly create a Phone List table that contains the first and last names of the donor, and the donor's home, work and fax phone numbers. You will then enter and sort the necessary data to print the list.

Hint

As you change from the Business to the Personal option buttons the list displayed in the Sample Table list box will change accordingly.

steps:

1. Create a new database called **Children's Council**, and use the Table Wizard to create a new table called **Phone List** that is based on the **Addresses** Sample Table, which is in the **Personal** Category
You now need to define the fields needed to hold the donors' names and numbers.

2. Select **AddressID** and rename it **ID**, select **FirstName**, select **LastName**, select **HomePhone** and rename it **Home**, select **WorkPhone** and rename it **Work**, then select **FaxNumber** and rename it **Fax**
Your table fields should match those shown in Figure P3-1.

3. Click **Next**, name the table **Phone List**, click **Next**, then click **Finish**
You now can enter the data for the phone list.

Hint

You can press [Enter] or [Tab] to move from field to field.

4. Maximize the Datasheet View window, then use Figure P3-2 to enter the 15 records for the Phone List table
Next, you want to sort the table by First Name, so the contact information will be easy to locate when you need it.

5. Sort the table by **First Name** in **Ascending** order
Your table should match the one shown in Figure P3-3.

6. Save the database table

FIGURE P3-1: **Field names for the Phone List table**

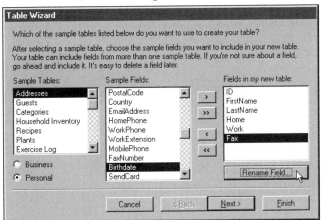

FIGURE P3-2: **Data records 1 to 15**

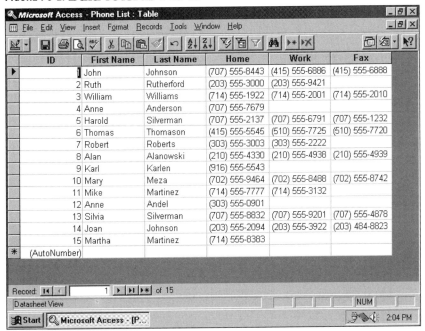

ID	First Name	Last Name	Home	Work	Fax
1	John	Johnson	(707) 555-8443	(415) 555-6886	(415) 555-6888
2	Ruth	Rutherford	(203) 555-3000	(203) 555-9421	
3	William	Williams	(714) 555-1922	(714) 555-2001	(714) 555-2010
4	Anne	Anderson	(707) 555-7679		
5	Harold	Silverman	(707) 555-2137	(707) 555-6791	(707) 555-1232
6	Thomas	Thomason	(415) 555-5545	(510) 555-7725	(510) 555-7720
7	Robert	Roberts	(303) 555-3003	(303) 555-2222	
8	Alan	Alanowski	(210) 555-4330	(210) 555-4938	(210) 555-4939
9	Karl	Karlen	(916) 555-5543		
10	Mary	Meza	(702) 555-9464	(702) 555-8488	(702) 555-8742
11	Mike	Martinez	(714) 555-7777	(714) 555-3132	
12	Anne	Andel	(303) 555-0901		
13	Silvia	Silverman	(707) 555-8832	(707) 555-9201	(707) 555-4878
14	Joan	Johnson	(203) 555-2094	(203) 555-3922	(203) 484-8823
15	Martha	Martinez	(714) 555-8383		

FIGURE P3-3: **Sorted Phone List**

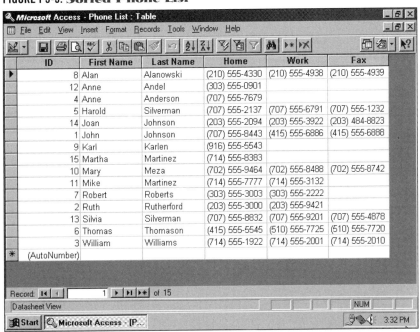

ID	First Name	Last Name	Home	Work	Fax
8	Alan	Alanowski	(210) 555-4330	(210) 555-4938	(210) 555-4939
12	Anne	Andel	(303) 555-0901		
4	Anne	Anderson	(707) 555-7679		
5	Harold	Silverman	(707) 555-2137	(707) 555-6791	(707) 555-1232
14	Joan	Johnson	(203) 555-2094	(203) 555-3922	(203) 484-8823
1	John	Johnson	(707) 555-8443	(415) 555-6886	(415) 555-6888
9	Karl	Karlen	(916) 555-5543		
15	Martha	Martinez	(714) 555-8383		
10	Mary	Meza	(702) 555-9464	(702) 555-8488	(702) 555-8742
11	Mike	Martinez	(714) 555-7777	(714) 555-3132	
7	Robert	Roberts	(303) 555-3003	(303) 555-2222	
2	Ruth	Rutherford	(203) 555-3000	(203) 555-9421	
13	Silvia	Silverman	(707) 555-8832	(707) 555-9201	(707) 555-4878
6	Thomas	Thomason	(415) 555-5545	(510) 555-7725	(510) 555-7720
3	William	Williams	(714) 555-1922	(714) 555-2001	(714) 555-2010

DONOR PHONE LIST FOR THE CHILDREN'S COUNCIL

You are almost ready to print the donor phone list in preparation for your trip. Increasing the font size to 12 points would make the list much easier to read, so you decide to make this change before printing the list.

activity:

Format and Print the Phone List

steps:

1. Show the **Formatting (Datasheet)** toolbar if necessary

You should now see the Formatting toolbar positioned directly above your table, as shown in Figure P3-4.

2. From the Edit menu, **Select All Records**, then select **12** from the **Font Size list arrow**

As you change the font size for the information shown in your table, the field widths do not adjust accordingly and need to be manually resized in order to list the data properly.

3. Adjust the widths of the fields to show the longest entry

Your table should match the one shown in Figure P3-5. Next, magnify the view in order to visually verify that the table will be printed correctly.

4. Print Preview the table then, using the **Zoom Control list arrow** resize the view to **75%**

Your table should match the one shown in the Print Preview in Figure P3-6.

Hint

You may need to resize the ID field.

5. If the layout shown on your screen does not fit on one page, adjust the field and field label widths as necessary

6. Print one copy of the Phone List table, then close Print Preview

You are returned to the Table View window.

7. Close the Phone List table and the Children's Council database, saving changes when prompted

FIGURE P3-4: **Changing the font size**

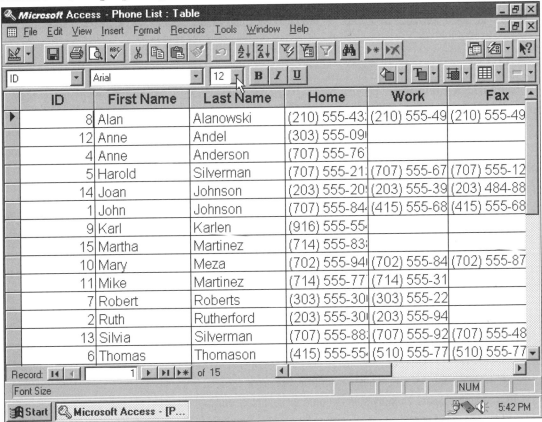

FIGURE P3-5: **Print Preview of Donor's Phone List**

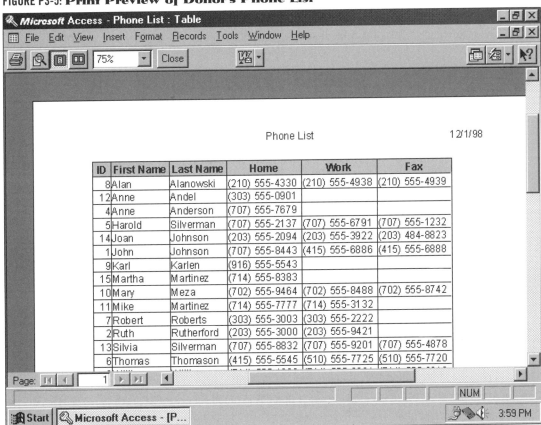

Independent Challenges

INDEPENDENT CHALLENGE 1

You are the head of the Pacific Coast Environmental Network, a non-profit organization that acts as a clearinghouse on issues of concern to its members, such as ecosystems, marine life, endangered species, ancient forests, vernal pools, and habitat restoration. To simplify the process of communicating with members, you decide to create a database that includes each member's mailing address and their primary issue of concern. After you build this database, you want to prepare a report that groups members by issue so that you can design a marketing brochure. You also need to print mailing labels so that you can send each member a copy of the brochure. You start by sketching out the structure of the Membership table.

Fields	Primary key

1. Create a database called "Environmental Network", then create the "Membership" table.
2. Create a member form with columnar layout that contains all the fields in the Membership table, and save it as "Member Issues".
3. In Form Design View, add a label box with the title "Environmental Network Member Issues" to the PageHeader section. Increase the font size and change the width of the label box to show the full title on the form.
4. In Form View, enter the names and addresses of 15 individuals and an issue of concern to them.
5. Create a report that is grouped by issue, sorted by last name, and in landscape orientation, and name it "Member Issues".
6. Preview the report, modify the report design to show the full contents of each label and text box, then print it.
7. Create mailing labels for all the members. Design a Prototype label for a standard mailing label that has three labels across and 10 labels down. Sort the labels first by Zip, then by City, and finally by Address.
8. Print a sheet of mailing labels, then close Report Design and the database.

INDEPENDENT CHALLENGE 2

As owner of Chapman & Chesney Advertising, you are always striving to develop client accounts. To aid you in this task, you decide to create a relational database that includes a table that lists client accounts and their current status ("Active" or "Inactive".) A second table will list client income for the last three years. After you create the database, you want to query it for some information that will help you to better understand and serve your clientele.

1. Start by outlining the structure of the two tables for the client database.

Tables	Fields	Primary keys
Accounts		
Income		

2. Create a relational database called "Chapman & Chesney", then create the "Accounts" table.
3. Enter data for 17 clients in the Accounts table, specifying "Inactive" for at least seven of the accounts.
4. Create the "Income" table. Choose the following relationship for the two tables: One record in the Income table will match one record in the Accounts table.

5. Enter income for a three-year period for the 17 clients that you specified in the Accounts table. Vary the income so that for most of the clients, income increases from year to year. For the other clients, show income as varying slightly or increasing and decreasing from year to year. The income range should vary from $15,000 for small clients up to $2,000,000 for large clients.
6. Use the Simple Query Wizard to create a Select Query that shows the Client name and account status fields from the accounts table and the income fields from the Income table.
7. Revise the query so that the income fields do not show in the query, add a Total Income field that adds the income for the three-year period, enter criteria that selects all Active accounts with less than $250,000 of total income and that also selects all Inactive Accounts, then run the query. *Hint*: To specify two conditions, list them on separate lines in the Criteria portion of the Design grid.
8. Create a custom report called "Client Development" that includes all the query fields, that groups clients by account status, and that lists clients in alphabetical order by client name.
9. Preview the report, make any adjustments to the report layout that you think will improve the appearance of the report, then print it.

INDEPENDENT CHALLENGE 3

Create a database that contains contact information for the group or event of your choice. For example, you might want to create a phone list for a club you belong to, or a contact sheet for an upcoming reunion or conference.

1. Create and name a database and then plan and create your contact list table. Spend some time planning the table structure. Use your imagination and your knowledge of Access to determine what types of information you might want to include. If, for example, you are creating a contact sheet for a sports club, you might want to include a field that shows each person's preferred practice time.
2. Based on your plan, create and name a table and enter at least 10 records.
3. Sort your table in a way that will make the table easy to use.
4. Format the table to increase the font and then print it.
5. Make a query based on the type on information the table contains. If, for example, your table contains information about a class reunion, you might create a query that shows which individuals have not yet indicated whether they plan to attend. If you need to create a related table or modify the existing table in order to elicit the information you need, do so.
6. Print a custom report based on your query results.

INDEPENDENT CHALLENGE 4

As an instructor for a local junior college, you have decided to put together a database that will help you track your past students, which classes they attended, and the final grades they received. You've decided to create a database consisting of two tables: a Student Master table and a Class History table. The Student Master table will contain data about the students, such as their student ID, their first and last names, and their phone numbers. The Class History table will contain data about what classes the students attended, such as the class name, the semester and year they took the class, and their final grade.

1. Create a database named "Student Data".
2. Create the "Student Master" and "Class History" tables and enter at least 10 records for each.
3. Create a query that will allow you to display all students that received a final grade of either a "B" or an "A."
4. Use the Report Wizard to create a report of the query results, sorted by last name, that groups all the classes a student has attended, and shows the semester and year he or she took the class (sorted in ascending order) and the final grade he or she received for each class.

Visual Workshop

Create a database called "Longevity", then create a table called "Longest Lives" using the data shown in Figure VW-1. Then create a custom report to match the one shown in Figure VW-2. Note that you will first need to make a query that filters the data so that only select records appear.

FIGURE VW-1: Longest Lives

Name	Nationality	Born	Died	Years	Days
Delin Filkins	United States	May 4, 1815	Dec 4, 1928	113	214
Pierre Joubert	Canada	Jul 15,1701	Nov 16, 1814	113	124
Shigechiyo Izumi	Japan	Jun 28, 1865	Jun 1, 1978	113	2
Katherine Plunket	Ireland	Nov 22, 1820	Oct 14, 1932	111	327
Johanna Booyson	South Africa	Jan 17, 1857	Jun 16, 1968	111	151
Margaret Neve	Channel Islands	May 18, 1792	Apr 4, 1903	110	321
Elizabeth Watkins	No. Ireland	Mar 10, 1863	Oct 31, 1973	110	234
Geert Boomgaard	Netherlands	Sep 23, 1788	Feb 3, 1899	110	113
Ada Sharp	Australia	Apr 6, 1861	May 15, 1971	110	39
Marie Flassayer	France	Jun 13, 1844	Apr 18, 1954	109	309
Rosalia Spoto	Italy	Aug 25, 1847	Feb 20, 1957	109	179
Rachel MacArthur	Scotland	Nov 26, 1827	Dec 10, 1936	109	14

FIGURE VW-2: Long-lived Persons report

Long-Lived Persons (Born on or After 1850)

Name	Born	Nationality	Died	Years	Days
Johanna Booyson	1/17/1857	South Africa	6/16/68	111	151
Ada Sharp	4/6/1861	Australia	5/15/71	110	39
Elizabeth Watkins	3/10/1863	No. Ireland	10/31/73	110	234

Microsoft
► Access
Projects

Employee Databases

In This Unit You Will Create:

 ► **Salary Increases Report**

 ► **Department Roster**

 ► **Employee Roster**

Microsoft Access is a valuable tool for tracking a wide variety of employee information, including such items as each individual's social security number, name, job title, department, hire date, salary, accrued vacation time, accrued sick leave, benefits, vesting in a retirement plan, home address, home telephone number, and emergency contacts. From an employee database, you can prepare salary, salary planning, merit increase, itemized benefits, performance appraisal, and emergency contacts reports as well as employee and telephone lists. ► In this unit you will learn how to use Access to create and work with employee databases. You will create relational and non-relational database tables with the Table Wizard and Design View, create queries with calculated fields, and create custom reports with summary totals.

Employee Salary Increases Report for Cerri Fabrics

Riya de Vries, the owner of Cerri Fabrics, wants to give her employees a merit increase for the upcoming year. Riya would like to give upper management a flat increase of $7,500 and give salaried workers an increase equal to 7.5% of their salary. She asks you to create a database table of her current employees, calculate their pay raise and new salary, and print a report on employee merit increases so that management can assess the impact of these salary increases on next year's budget.

Project Activities

Create an Employee Database

Riya wants you to include each employee's social security number, name, job title, hire date, current salary, and employment status in the employee database table. For the employment status field, use a code to distinguish between upper management and salaried employees.

Create a Query with Calculated Fields

After defining the database table and entering information for Riya's current employees, you will create a select query that calculates a merit increase based on employment status and that also calculates each employee's new salary.

Create a Salary Increases Report

Next you will create a custom report that lists employees in order by name and shows each employee's name, title, salary, merit increase, and new salary.

Customize the Salary Increases Report

Riya also asked you to include a grand total for salaries, merit increases, and new salary levels so that she knows how the new salary increases affect the company's bottom line.

When you have completed Project 1, your report will appear similar to the one in Figure P1-1.

Employee Salary Increases

Last Name	First Name	Title	Salary	Merit	New Salary
Chalupsky	Craig	Administrative Assistant	$32,300	$2,423	$34,723
Chamberlain	Julio	Production Worker	$27,390	$2,054	$29,444
Chen	Chuen Sing	Secretary	$41,600	$3,120	$44,720
Chiotti	Murray	Purchasing Manager	$72,000	$7,500	$79,500
Chojnacki	Gail	Production Manager	$51,400	$7,500	$58,900
Cole	Marianna	Production Worker	$32,000	$2,400	$34,400
Filardo	Nora	Secretary	$35,000	$2,625	$37,625
Hasse	Chas	Vice President	$100,000	$7,500	$107,500
Lamar	Jayson	Production Worker	$36,500	$2,738	$39,238
Logasa	Val	Bookkeeper	$45,200	$3,390	$48,590
Maslyn-Colyer	Terri	Executive Secretary	$49,900	$3,743	$53,643
Moreno	Aurora	Production Worker	$39,700	$2,978	$42,678
Okamoto	Melissa	Production Worker	$33,300	$2,498	$35,798
Ramos	Maria	Accountant	$67,800	$7,500	$75,300
Rossner	Rosemary	President	$250,000	$7,500	$257,500
Totals			$914,090	$65,467	$979,557

PROJECT 1

activity:

Create an Employee Database

Your first step is to create the employee database tables so that you can calculate the new salary. You will use the Table Wizard to create the basic table, and then use Design View to add another field and adjust field properties.

steps:

1. Start Access, create a database named **Cerri Fabrics**, open the **Table Wizard**, then click **Employees** in the Sample Tables list box

   This sample table will provide all the fields you need except for the employment status field.

2. Double-click **SocialSecurityNumber** in the Sample Fields list, click **Rename Field**, rename the field to **SSN**, double-click **FirstName**, double-click **LastName**, double-click **Title**, double-click **Salary**, double-click **DateHired** and rename it **HireDate**, then click **Next**

   Although you want to use the name Access suggests for the table, you want to select the primary key.

3. Click the **No, I'll set the primary key option button**, then click **Next**

   You want to use the SNN field as the primary key.

Hint

You do not need to enter dashes in the SSN (social security number) field or a dollar sign in the Salary field, because Access will automatically enter them for you. However, if you do enter the dashes and dollar sign, Access will not insert two copies of each symbol. Rather, it will recognize them as formatting symbols that, in some cases, separate groups of digits.

4. Make sure the SSN field and the data option "Numbers and/or letters I enter when I add records" are highlighted, click **Next**, click the **Modify the table design option button**, then click **Finish**

   First, you want to modify the properties of the Salary field.

5. Maximize the Design View window, click the **Salary field row selector**, click the **Decimal Places cell** on the General Field Properties sheet, click the **Decimal Places list arrow**, then click **0**

   Next add the Status field and define its properties.

6. Click in the next available cell in the Field Name column, type **Status**, press **[Enter]**, click the **Data Type list arrow** for the Status field, click **Number**, click the **Field Size cell** on the General Field Properties sheet, click the **Field Size list arrow**, then click **Integer**

   Now you are ready to save your changes to the table structure and enter employee data.

7. Switch to **Datasheet View** and enter the employee data shown in Figure P1-2

8. Save the table

FIGURE P1-2: **Data for records 1 to 15 of the Employees table**

Microsoft Access - [Employees : Table]

File Edit View Insert Format Records Tools Window Help

SSN	First Name	Last Name	Title	Salary	HireDate	Status
218-98-6537	Craig	Chalupsky	Administrative Assistant	$32,300	1/10/96	2
287-48-3671	Terri	Maslyn-Colyer	Executive Secretary	$49,900	6/15/89	2
357-29-7351	Jayson	Lamar	Production Worker	$36,500	7/31/85	2
398-65-5386	Chuen Sing	Chen	Secretary	$41,600	8/17/88	2
453-82-7638	Melissa	Okamoto	Production Worker	$33,300	11/20/89	2
464-28-3949	Aurora	Moreno	Production Worker	$39,700	5/1/84	2
479-86-7432	Gail	Chojnacki	Production Manager	$51,400	4/23/86	1
524-01-7429	Murray	Chiotti	Purchasing Manager	$72,000	12/3/95	1
527-38-2937	Nora	Filardo	Secretary	$35,000	2/19/95	2
533-21-3495	Chas	Hasse	Vice President	$100,000	10/27/91	1
563-91-8762	Rosemary	Rossner	President	$250,000	3/21/81	1
639-33-6848	Maria	Ramos	Accountant	$67,800	9/22/87	1
671-22-3892	Val	Logasa	Bookkeeper	$45,200	4/9/90	2
781-53-2671	Julio	Chamberlain	Production Worker	$27,390	7/11/92	2
783-82-9623	Marianna	Cole	Production Worker	$32,000	6/1/87	2
						0

Clues to Use

Planning ahead

Personnel and Human Resources departments need to produce a wide variety of personnel and employee reports to provide both management and employees with information on their employment, pay, and benefits. Therefore, it is important to plan the structure of your employee database in advance, so that you are later able to produce all of the types of reports that you need.

activity:

Create a Query with Calculated Fields

Next you will create a select query with the Simple Query Wizard and add two calculated fields to the query. One calculated field will compute the merit increase and the other the employee's new salary. For the merit increase field, you will use the IIf function to examine the entry in the Status field of the underlying table and determine whether the employee gets a flat salary increase of $7,500 or a percentage increase of 7.5%.

Access 7 Users

If you are using Access 7.0, click the **New Object button** list arrow, click **New Query**, then double-click **Simple Query Wizard**

steps:

1. Click the **New Object button list arrow** on the Table Datasheet toolbar, click **Query**, then double-click **Simple Query Wizard**

   You want to include all the fields except the SSN, HireDate, and Status fields in the query.

2. Double-click **FirstName**, double-click **LastName**, double-click **Title**, double-click **Salary**, then click **Next**

   You want to see the table detail in the query and then add calculated fields to the query, which will involve modifying the design.

3. Click the **Detail option button** (if necessary), click **Next**, click the **Modify the query design option button**, then click **Finish**

   To construct the first calculated field, which requires the IIf function, you decide to use Expression Builder.

4. Click the empty **Field cell** in the column to the right of the Salary field cell, click the **Build button** on the Query Design toolbar, type **Merit:** as the field name in the Expression Box, double-click the **Functions folder** in the Expression Elements list box on the left, click the **Built-In Functions folder**, scroll and then click **Program Flow** in the Categories list box in the center, then double-click **IIf** in the Functions list box on the right

   Access adds the IIf function to the Expression Box and identifies the arguments you need to specify.

5. Click **<<Expr>>**, press **[Delete]**, click **<<expr>>**, type **[Status]=1**, click **<<truepart>>**, type **7500**, click **<<falsepart>>**, type **[Salary]*.075**, as shown in Figure P1-3, then click **OK**

   Now you want to add a calculated field to calculate the new salary level. This time, you'll enter the expression directly in the query form.

Trouble

If Access informs you that there is a problem with the expression, click OK, open Expression Builder again, correct the problem, then click OK to save your changes. Make sure you did not omit the required punctuation and that you did not include any extra punctuation, such as commas.

6. In the design grid, click the empty **Field cell** in the column after the Merit Field cell, type **New Salary: [Salary]+[Merit]** then click the **Run button** on the Query Design toolbar

   After viewing the results, you decide to format the calculated values consistently.

7. Switch to Design View, click the **Merit Field cell**, click the **Properties button** on the Query Design toolbar, click the **Format list box** on the General property sheet, click the **Format list arrow**, scroll and click **Currency**, click the **Decimal Places list box**, click the **Decimal Places list arrow**, click **0**, close the Field Properties dialog box, then make the same change for the New Salary field

   Now you can run and then save the updated query.

8. Click the **Run button** on the Query Design toolbar, then save the updated query

   Figure P1-4 shows the updated query with the calculated results for the Merit and New Salary fields.

FIGURE P1-3: **Completed IIf function for the Merit calculated field**

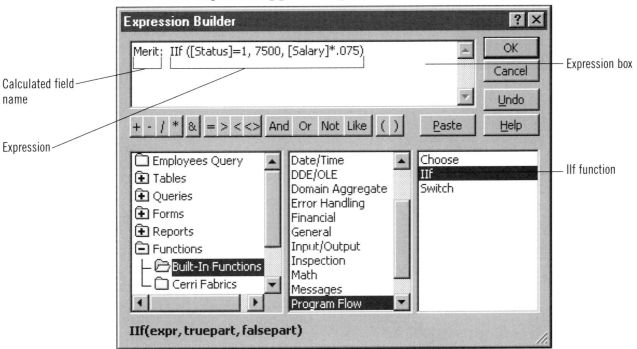

Calculated field name

Expression

Expression box

IIf function

IIf(expr, truepart, falsepart)

FIGURE P1-4: **Updated query with calculated merit increases and new salary levels**

First Name	Last Name	Title	Salary	Merit	New Salary
Craig	Chalupsky	Administrative Assistant	$32,300	$2,423	$34,723
Terri	Maslyn-Colyer	Executive Secretary	$49,900	$3,743	$53,643
Jayson	Lamar	Production Worker	$36,500	$2,738	$39,238
Chuen Sing	Chen	Secretary	$41,600	$3,120	$44,720
Melissa	Okamoto	Production Worker	$33,300	$2,498	$35,798
Aurora	Moreno	Production Worker	$39,700	$2,978	$42,678
Gail	Chojnacki	Production Manager	$51,400	$7,500	$58,900
Murray	Chiotti	Purchasing Manager	$72,000	$7,500	$79,500
Nora	Filardo	Secretary	$35,000	$2,625	$37,625
Chas	Hasse	Vice President	$100,000	$7,500	$107,500
Rosemary	Rossner	President	$250,000	$7,500	$257,500
Maria	Ramos	Accountant	$67,800	$7,500	$75,300
Val	Logasa	Bookkeeper	$45,200	$3,390	$48,590
Julio	Chamberlain	Production Worker	$27,390	$2,054	$29,444
Marianna	Cole	Production Worker	$32,000	$2,400	$34,400

Calculated fields

Clues to Use

Building an expression

To build an expression, replace the placeholders in chevrons with the arguments that the function requires. In the IIf function, for example, you replace the <<Expr>> placeholder with the field name, the <<expr>> placeholder with the expression or condition to test, the <<truepart>> placeholder with the formula or value to use if the condition is true, and the <<falsepart>> placeholder with the formula or value to use if the condition is false.

activity:

Create a Salary Increases Report

Next you will use the Report Wizard to create a report from the query. The report will list employees in order by name and show each employee's name, title, salary, merit increase, and new salary.

Access 7 Users

If you are using Access 7.0, click the **New Object** button, click **New Report,** then double-click **Report Wizard**

Hint

As you build reports, experiment with different grouping and sort options. You might discover a new report format that lists the information in a more useful format.

steps:

1. Click the **New Object button** on the Query Datasheet toolbar, click **Report**, then double-click **Report Wizard**

You want to include all the fields from the query in the report.

2. Click the **Select All Fields button**, then click **Next**

You do not need to group the report detail, but you do want to arrange employees alphabetically by name.

3. Click **Next**, click the **1 list arrow**, click **LastName**, click the **2 list arrow**, click **FirstName**, then click **Next**

You decide to use the Tabular layout, landscape orientation, and the Bold style.

4. In the Layout area, click the **Tabular option button** to select it (if necessary), click **Landscape** in the Orientation area, click the **Adjust the field width so all fields fit on a page check box** to select it (if necessary), click **Next**, click **Bold** when prompted for the style, then click **Next**

After naming the report, you want to preview it.

5. Type **Employee Salary Increases** in the report name box, click the **Preview the report option button** (if necessary), then click **Finish**

After examining the report in the Print Preview window, as shown in Figure P1-5, you remember that Riya also wanted you to include totals for the Merit and New Salary fields.

6. Click **Close** on the Print Preview Toolbar

Access switches to Report Design View so that you can modify the layout of the report.

FIGURE P1-5: **Preview of the Employee Salary Increases report**

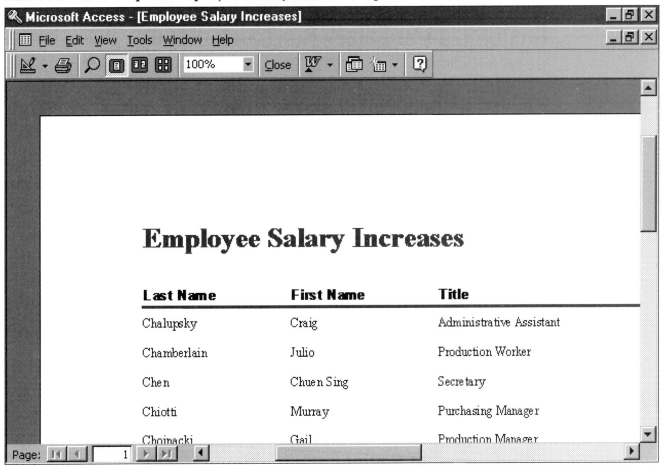

activity:

Customize the Salary Increases Report

In the Report Footer section of the report, you need to include text boxes with an expression that uses the Sum function to calculate a grand total for salaries, merit increases, and new salary levels.

steps:

1. Adjust your view so that you can see the New Salary label and text boxes, click the **Text Box button** abl on the Toolbox toolbar, then click in the blank **Report Footer section** below the New Salary text box

   Access adds a control to the Report Footer section. Next you want to change the label in the label box.

2. Click the **label box** for the new control, click the **Properties button** on the Report Design toolbar, type **Totals** in the Caption text box of the Format tab of the Label dialog box, then close the Label dialog box

   Since this label will identify all three totals Riya wants for assessing the bottom line, you decide to move the label box to the left side of the report and align it with the FirstName label box.

Trouble

If the label and text boxes move together, click the Undo button , click the label box, then repeat Step 3.

3. Point to the move handle of the label box and when the pointer changes to 👆, as shown in Figure P1-6, drag the label box to the left side of the Report Footer section, release the mouse button, press and hold [Shift] while you click the **LastName label box**, click **Format** on the menu bar, point to **Align**, then click **Left**

   Now enter an expression that calculates a total for the New Salary text box and specify its format.

Access 7 Users

You will find the Decimal Places list box on the Data tab rather than the Format tab.

4. Scroll right and click the **text box** with the label "Unbound" in the Report Footer section, click the **Properties button** on the Report Design toolbar, click the **Data tab** in the Text Box dialog box, type **=sum([New Salary])** in the Control Source list box, click the **Format tab**, click the **Format list box**, click the **Format list arrow**, scroll and click **Currency**, click in the **Decimal Places list box**, click the **Decimal Places list arrow**, click **0**, then close the Text Box dialog box

   Now you can align this control with the New Salary text box.

5. Press and hold [Shift] while you click the **New Salary text box** in the Detail section, click **Format** on the menu bar, point to **Align**, then click **Right**

   Figure P1-7 shows the text box with the expression. Next you want to define the same types of controls for the Merit and Salary fields, but you do not need the label boxes for these calculated controls.

6. Repeat the same process to create another unbound text box in the Report Footer section, click and delete the associated label box, enter an expression for the text box that calculates a grand total for the merit amounts, select a currency format with no decimal places, and align the text box with the label box that shows the report detail, then repeat the same steps to create a text box that calculates the total salary

   Now you can preview your report, make any last minute changes, then save and print it.

FIGURE P1-6: **Moving the label box for the control that will
calculate a total**

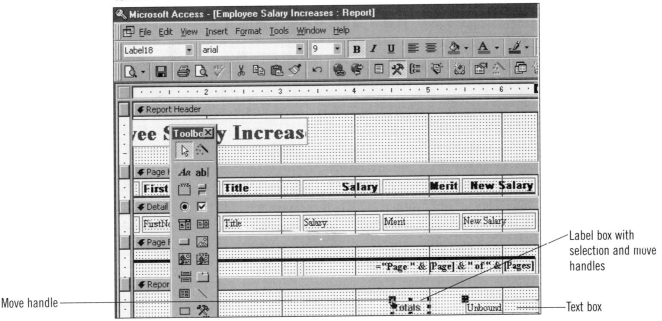

Move handle

Label box with
selection and move
handles

Text box

FIGURE P1-7: **Text box for calculating a grand total**

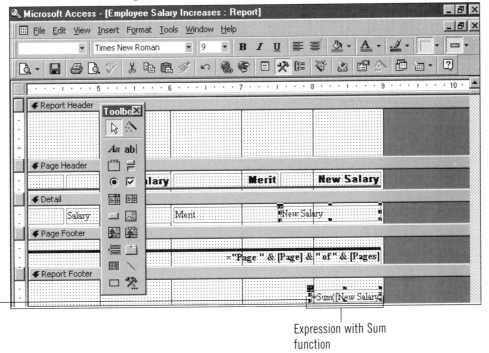

Text box in Report
Footer section

Expression with Sum
function

Clues to Use

Controls

Access uses controls, or graphical objects, to identify the location and features of titles, headings, report detail, summary data, headers, footers, and lines on a report. Report controls might display the contents of a table or query field, contain text or numbers, use expressions such as formulas or functions to calculate values, or insert special features, such as the date and page number, on a report. A bound control is linked to a specific table or query field and shows the data in that field in a previewed or printed report. In contrast, an unbound control, such as a report title or a text box with an expression that calculates a total, is not tied to the underlying table. You can select, format, move, resize, and copy controls to enhance the appearance of data in a report.

Department Roster for California Mutual

California Mutual, an insurance company, specializes in providing healthcare insurance for small businesses. Andy Gillman, the vice president of Human Resources, would like to provide the organization's department heads with a concise listing of all persons employed by California Mutual. Mr. Gillman has asked you, a senior analyst with the company's information systems department, to develop a system that will allow him to track employee information such as name, social security number, the date each employee started working, and the department each employee works in. He would also like you to produce a report, grouped by department and sorted alphabetically by employee name, that he can issue to all department managers as needed. To accomplish these tasks, you will **design and enter data for two related database tables, modify and update a database table, create a new related table, create a query,** and then **print a custom report.**

activity:

Design and Enter Data for Two Related Database Tables

You will create a database and, using Design View, define two tables: the Employee Master table and the Department Master table. The first table will be used to maintain basic employee demographic data such as the employees' first and last names, their social security number, their start date, and the ID for the department in which they work. The second table will provide the name for each department.

steps:

Hint

You can designate a primary key while in Design View by selecting the desired field and clicking the Primary Key button 🔑 on the Table Design toolbar.

1. Create a new database based on the **Blank Database template**, and save it as **Mutual Insurance** to the location where you are saving your files for this book
   First you'll design the Employee Master table.

2. Using Design View, create the table shown in Figure P2-1
   Having designed the Employee Master table, you can now enter the data for this table.

3. Save the table as **Employee Master**, switch to **Datasheet View**, enter the data shown in Figure P2-2, then save the table
   Your table should resemble the one shown in Figure P2-2. You are now ready to create the second table.

4. Using Design View, create the table shown in Figure P2-3
   This table will be used to identify the department and the department manager. Your completed design should match the one shown in Figure P2-3.

Time To
✓ Save
✓ Close

5. Save the table as **Department Master**, switch to **Datasheet View**, then enter the data as shown in Figure P2-4
   Your table should resemble the one shown in Figure P2-4.

FIGURE P2-1: Employee Master table in Design View

Microsoft Access - [Employee Master : Table]

File   Edit   View   Insert   Tools   Window   Help

Field Name	Data Type	Description
⑧ Employee ID	AutoNumber	Primary Key
L Name	Text	
F Name	Text	
SSN	Text	Employee's Social Security Number
Start Date	Date/Time	Date Employee started with Company
Dept ID	Number	Employee's Department ID

FIGURE P2-2: Data for records 1 to 15 of the Employee Master table

Microsoft Access - [Employee Master : Table]

File   Edit   View   Insert   Format   Records   Tools   Window   Help

Employee ID	L Name	F Name	SSN	Start Date	Dept ID
1	Johnson	Gloria	123-45-6789	2/4/95	10
2	Miller	Ralph	234-56-7890	9/23/95	30
3	O'Brian	Patrick	345-67-8901	10/1/95	20
4	Sanchez	Jose	456-78-9012	12/15/95	30
5	Washington	Leroy	567-89-0123	1/10/96	10
6	Martinez	Berta	678-90-1234	4/1/96	30
7	Chan	Charles	901-23-4567	5/1/96	50
8	Rubal	Venkatesh	012-34-5678	5/1/97	20
9	Rondowski	Boris	098-76-5432	5/15/97	20
10	Anton	Julia	987-65-4321	8/1/97	10
11	Martini	Lucia	876-54-3210	11/4/97	50
12	Thompson	William	765-43-2109	1/7/98	40
13	Carpenter	Joseph	654-32-1098	3/4/98	40
14	Fugimoto	Lloyd	543-21-0987	6/17/98	50
15	Reed	David	432-10-9876	7/1/98	50
(AutoNumber)					0

FIGURE P2-3: Department Master table in Design View

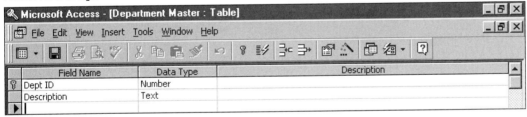

Microsoft Access - [Department Master : Table]

File   Edit   View   Insert   Tools   Window   Help

Field Name	Data Type	Description
⑧ Dept ID	Number	
Description	Text	

FIGURE P2-4: Data for records 1 to 5 of the Department Master table

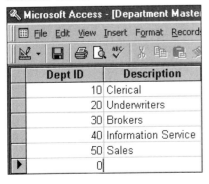

Microsoft Access - [Department Master]

File   Edit   View   Insert   Format   Records

Dept ID	Description
10	Clerical
20	Underwriters
30	Brokers
40	Information Service
50	Sales
0	

activities:

Modify a Table, Update Data, and Create a Table

Upon reviewing the Employee Master table design, Mr. Gillman would like you to add an additional field to the Employee Master table: an employee's job code ID number. To do so, you will need to add an additional field to the Employee Master using Design View, update the Employee Master, and then create a new table named Job Codes that describes what the codes represent.

steps:

1. From the Tables tab, select the **Employee Master table**, then click **Design**

In Design View, you can add the new Job Code ID field.

2. Click the first blank cell in the Field Name column, type **Job Code ID**, set the Data Type as **Number**, then type **Employee's Job Code** as the Description

Your modified table design should match the one shown in Figure P2-5. You can now update data in the Employee Master table.

3. Switch to **Datasheet View**, then update the data for the Employee Master table as shown in Figure P2-6

Your table should match the one shown in Figure P2-6.

4. Save the table, then close it

Next, you will create the Job Codes table.

5. From the Tables tab, click **New** and using Design View create the table shown in Figure P2-7

Your table should match the one shown in Figure P2-7.

6. Switch to **Datasheet View**, save the table as **Job Codes**, then enter the data as shown in Figure P2-8

Your table should match the one shown in Figure P2-8.

7. Save, then close the table

FIGURE P2-5: Modified Employee Master table design

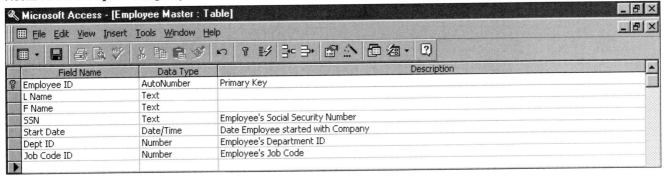

Field Name	Data Type	Description
🔑 Employee ID	AutoNumber	Primary Key
L Name	Text	
F Name	Text	
SSN	Text	Employee's Social Security Number
Start Date	Date/Time	Date Employee started with Company
Dept ID	Number	Employee's Department ID
Job Code ID	Number	Employee's Job Code

FIGURE P2-6: Updated Employee Master table

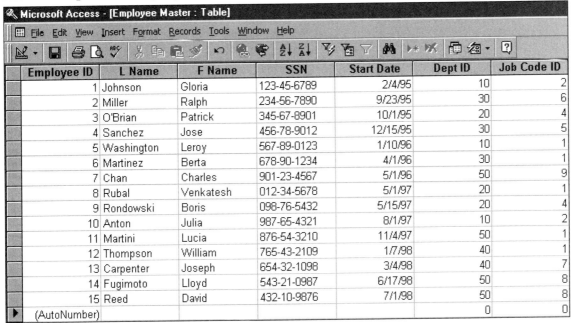

Employee ID	L Name	F Name	SSN	Start Date	Dept ID	Job Code ID
1	Johnson	Gloria	123-45-6789	2/4/95	10	2
2	Miller	Ralph	234-56-7890	9/23/95	30	6
3	O'Brian	Patrick	345-67-8901	10/1/95	20	4
4	Sanchez	Jose	456-78-9012	12/15/95	30	5
5	Washington	Leroy	567-89-0123	1/10/96	10	1
6	Martinez	Berta	678-90-1234	4/1/96	30	1
7	Chan	Charles	901-23-4567	5/1/96	50	9
8	Rubal	Venkatesh	012-34-5678	5/1/97	20	1
9	Rondowski	Boris	098-76-5432	5/15/97	20	4
10	Anton	Julia	987-65-4321	8/1/97	10	2
11	Martini	Lucia	876-54-3210	11/4/97	50	1
12	Thompson	William	765-43-2109	1/7/98	40	1
13	Carpenter	Joseph	654-32-1098	3/4/98	40	7
14	Fugimoto	Lloyd	543-21-0987	6/17/98	50	8
15	Reed	David	432-10-9876	7/1/98	50	8
(AutoNumber)					0	0

FIGURE P2-7: Job Codes table in Design View

Field Name	Data Type	Description
🔑 Job Code ID	Number	
Job Code Description	Text	

FIGURE P2-8: Data for records 1 to 9 of the Job Codes table

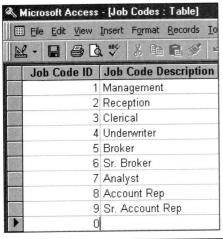

Job Code ID	Job Code Description
1	Management
2	Reception
3	Clerical
4	Underwriter
5	Broker
6	Sr. Broker
7	Analyst
8	Account Rep
9	Sr. Account Rep
0	

activities:

Define Relationships, Create a Query, then Create a Custom Report

To produce the report Mr. Gillman has requested, you will need to establish relationships between the tables you have created, create a query, and then create a custom report grouped by department that lists the required employee information.

steps:

Hint

Dragging fields from one table to another while in the Relationships window links the two tables together. Linked tables must have a duplicate field in both tables. It's a good idea to have only one linking field with the same field name in both tables.

1. Click the **Relationships button** 🔲 on the Table Database toolbar, add the **Department Master**, **Employee Master**, and **Job Codes** tables to the Relationships window, then close the Show Table dialog box

2. Drag the **Dept ID** field from the **Employee Master table** to the **Dept ID** field in the **Department Master table**, accepting the default relationship, then drag the **Job Code ID** field from the **Employee Master table** to the **Job Code ID** field in the **Job Codes table**, accepting the default relationships

Your screen should resemble the one shown in Figure P2-9.

3. From the Queries tab, create a new query using the **Simple Query Wizard**

4. From the Employee Master table select **Employee ID**, **F Name**, **L Name**, **SSN**, and **Dept ID**; from the Department Master table select **Description**; from the Employee Master table again select **Job Code ID**; from the Job Codes table select **Job Code Description**; click **Next**, click the **Detail option button**, if necessary click **Next**, name the query **Department Roster**, then click **Finish**

5. Switch to **Query Design View**, then select the fields **L Name** and **Dept ID** to sort in ascending order

6. Click the **Run button** ❗ on the Query Design toolbar, then save and close the table

7. From the Reports tab, create a new report using **Report Wizard**

8. Select all the fields from the **Department Roster** query, view the data by **Employee Master**, group the report by **Dept ID** and then by **Description**, sort the report in **ascending order** by **L Name**, select the default settings for orientation and field width, choose the **Corporate** style, name the report **Department Roster List**, click the **Preview the report option button** (if necessary), click **Finish**, then use the report Design View to modify your report to resemble the one shown in Figure P2-10

9. Print the report, then save and close the report and the databases

FIGURE P2-9: **Table relationships**

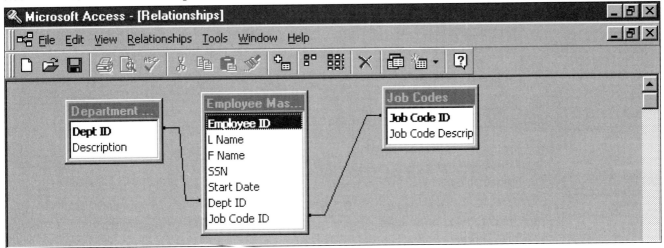

FIGURE P2-10: **Department Roster List**

Department Roster List

Department	Employee ID	Employee Name		SSN	Job Code	
10						
Clerical						
	10	Julia	Anton	987-65-4321	2	Reception
	1	Gloria	Johnson	123-45-6789	2	Reception
	6	Leroy	Washington	567-89-0123	1	Management
20						
Underwriters						
	3	Patrick	O'Brian	345-67-8901	4	Underwriter
	9	Boris	Rondowski	098-76-5432	4	Underwriter
	8	Venkatesh	Rubal	012-34-5678	1	Management
30						
Brokers						
	6	Berta	Martinez	678-90-1234	1	Management
	2	Ralph	Miller	234-56-7890	6	Sr. Broker
	4	Jose	Sanchez	456-78-9012	5	Broker
40						
Information Service						
	13	Joseph	Carpenter	654-32-1098	7	Analyst
	12	William	Thompson	765-43-2109	1	Management
50						
Sales						
	7	Charles	Chan	901-23-4567	9	Sr. Account Rep
	14	Lloyd	Fugimoto	543-21-0987	8	Account Rep
	11	Lucia	Martini	876-54-3210	1	Management
	15	David	Reed	432-10-9876	8	Account Rep

Page 1 of 1

Employee Roster for Baker Security

Tom Baker, owner of a small security firm, specializes in providing services for the entertainment industry. Recently, Baker Security has began the process of reviewing its employees salaries against the average salaries for similar jobs in the surrounding geographic area. As part of this analysis, Mr. Baker has asked you, his office manager, to create a report listing all employees hired after December 31, 1997, showing their pay step and rate. To do so, you will **create a database, design and enter data for two tables, define a relationship between the tables, create a query,** and then **develop a custom report**.

activities:

Create a Database and Design and Enter Data for Two Tables

steps:

1. Create a new database called **Baker Security** and use Design View to create the table shown in Figure P3-1
   Make sure to designate the Employee ID field as the primary key. Now you are ready to enter data in this table.

2. Switch to **Datasheet View** and save the table as **Employee Roster**

3. Using Figure P3-2, enter the data for the Employee Roster table, save the table, then close it
   When you have finished entering the data, your table should match the one shown in Figure P3-2.

4. Create a table named **Rate Master** as shown in Figure P3-3, designating the **Rate ID** field as the primary key

5. Complete the table by entering the data shown in Figure P3-4

6. Save and close the Rate Master table

FIGURE P3-1: **Design View for Employee Roster table**

FIGURE P3-2: **Data for records 1 to 10 of the Employee Roster table**

Employee ID	Last Name	First Name	Date of Hire	Pay Step
1	Smith	Sue	3/16/97	10
2	Brown	Andy	7/1/97	7
3	Jimenez	Pepe	9/15/97	9
4	Jones	Tim	11/21/97	8
5	Nunez	Andria	12/1/97	6
6	Adams	Sam	2/15/98	7
7	Davis	Bob	3/1/98	5
8	Jones	Buck	3/15/98	5
9	Martin	Sue	5/1/98	3
10	Smith	Joe	6/21/98	1
(AutoNumber)				0

FIGURE P3-3: **Rate Master table in Design View**

FIGURE P3-4: **Data for records 1 to 10 of the Rate Master table**

Rate ID	Amount
1	$10.00
2	$10.50
3	$11.00
4	$11.50
5	$12.00
6	$12.50
7	$13.00
8	$13.50
9	$14.00
10	$14.50
(AutoNumber)	$0.00

activities:

Link Tables, Create a Query, and Produce a Custom Report

As part of his salary review, Mr. Baker would like to see a report, sorted in descending order of hire date, of all employees hired after December 31, 1997. He would like the report to list the employee's name, their employee ID number, the date on which they were hired, and their current pay step and rate. To provide Mr. Baker with this information, you will link the Employee Roster and Rate Master tables, create a query, and develop a custom report.

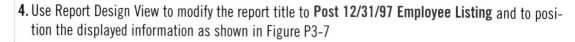

Hint

You can link files even though their field names do not match so long as the field data type is the same and the data represents the same type of information.

Hint

You can toggle between descending and ascending sort order by clicking the Sort Ascending button  next to the field list box when prompted by Report Wizard about what sort order you want for your records.

steps:

1. Link the **Employee Roster** and **Rate Master** tables using the **Rate ID** and **Pay Step** fields, as shown in Figure P3-5, then close the Relationships window

2. Using the **Simple Query Wizard**, create a new query named **Employees Hired After 12/31/97** as shown in Figure P3-6

3. Using **Report Wizard**, create a new report based on the **Employees Hired After 12/31/97** query. Accept the default view and grouping options, sort the report in **descending order** of **Date of Hire** and choose the default formatting options and the **Corporate** style, then save the report

4. Use Report Design View to modify the report title to **Post 12/31/97 Employee Listing** and to position the displayed information as shown in Figure P3-7

5. Print the report, then save your work and close the query and the database

Clues to Use

Formatting Date/Time elements

To use a date in an expression in a Design grid, you must insert number signs (#) around it. This indicates to Access that the element is a date/time value. If the field was defined as a Date/Time data type when the table was designed, then you can type the value in any common date or time format and Access will automatically insert the # signs around the value.

FIGURE P3-5: **Relationship between Employee Roster and Rate Master tables**

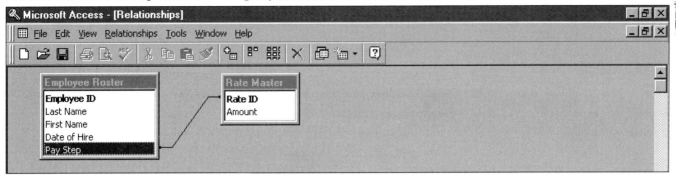

FIGURE P3-6: **Employee Hired After 12/31/97 query in Query Design View**

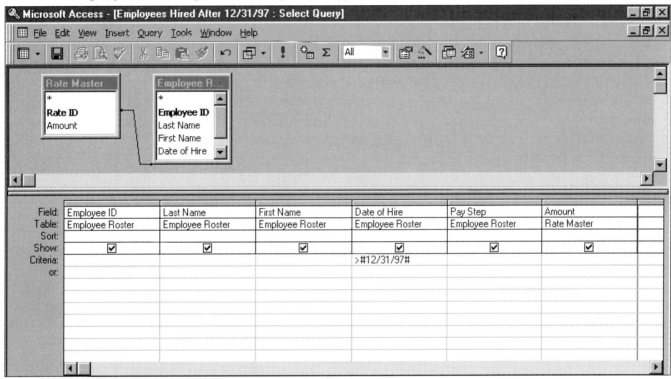

FIGURE P3-7: **Post 12/31/97 Employee Listing in Print Preview**

Independent Challenges

INDEPENDENT CHALLENGE 1

As owner and senior partner of Nolan, Chandler, Tabor, Houston & Stolpe, you want to give each of your associate attorneys a bonus equal to 25% of their salary and your support staff a bonus equal to 12.5% of their annual salary. You decide to create a database table to calculate this year's bonuses for the two different groups of employees.

1. Use the worksheet below to plan the fields needed for the table, the calculated fields for the query, and the fields needed for the report:

   Table fields: ....
   Calculated fields for the query: ....
   Report fields: ....

2. Create a database called "Nolan & Associates," and then create a table named "Employees." Then enter data for yourself and a staff of ten.
   Hint: (Law firms typically have a senior partner who owns the firm, associate partners who invest in the firm, paralegals to research cases, an office manager, legal secretaries, and a receptionist.)
3. Create a query in which you calculate each employee's bonus and their total income.
4. Create a report called "Partner and Employee Bonuses" that shows the results of your query and includes grand totals for salaries, bonuses, and total income, then print your report.

INDEPENDENT CHALLENGE 2

You are the owner of TriCounty Temps, an agency that places temporary word-processing employees on short- and long-term assignments. To meet the needs of your clients, you want to create a relational database that tracks the skill level, hourly pay, and availability of each of your temporary employees.

1. Plan the structure of your relational database and the relationship of the tables by filling in the worksheet below. Consider using one table to keep track of individual employees and their hourly pay, and another to track skill levels.

Tables:	Fields	Primary Key	Linking Field
Employees:	....	....	....
	....	....	....
Skill Levels:	....	....	....

2. Create a relational database called TriCounty Temps, define the structure of each table, then enter data for 15 temporary employees in one table, and data for at least four skill levels within the other table.
3. Create a query that shows the rate of pay, skill level, and availability of all your temporary employees.
4. From the query, create a report called "Temporary Employees" that organizes temps by skill level, by availability, and then by employee name.
5. Enhance the appearance of the report, then print it.

INDEPENDENT CHALLENGE 3

As the owner of Southbay Contracting, you have been asked by your staff to evaluate the firm's healthcare benefits package. Southbay currently offers its employees an option of three health plans, two dental plans, and two vision plans. Employees may elect one option from each group. You've decided to create a database with two tables: an Employee Electives table and a Benefits Master table. From these tables, you would like to create a report listing the employee's ID, the employee's name, and the three health plan options they have chosen.

1. Create a database called "Health Plan." This database will contain two related tables, one to maintain the employees health care elective codes and the other to provide a description of those electives.
2. Create a table called "Benefits Master." You will use this table to identify the Plan ID codes and descriptions. Decide how you will structure the table, and how you will code and name each plan, using the worksheet below:

Fields: ....

Plan names and codes: ....

3. Develop and enter data for three health, two dental, and two vision plans in the Benefits Master table.
4. Create a table called "Employee Electives" that includes fields for the employees ID, first and last names, and code fields for three healthcare electives.
5. Develop and enter data for 10 employees into the Employee Electives table, then link this table to the Benefits Master table.
6. Create a report, sorted by the employee's last name, that lists the employee and the descriptions of their healthcare plan options.
7. Format the report attractively, then print one copy of it.

INDEPENDENT CHALLENGE 4

As the senior partner of a midsized management consulting firm, it is your responsibility to determine this year's employee profit sharing amounts and provide your junior partners with a report of this information. After some thought, you have decided to give them each 10% of the revenue, less their annual base salary, that they have brought into the firm over the last year.

1. Create a database named "Profit Sharing."
2. Create a table named "Data." You will use this table to maintain data such as the partners' names, their salary, and the amount of revenue they brought into the firm over the year. Decide how you will structure this table, and what information you will need to maintain in order to produce the necessary report. Fill in the worksheet below with the necessary information:

Fields: ....

Calculation needed to determine profit sharing: ....

3. Develop and enter data for 15 partners.
4. Create a query that will allow you to calculate the profit sharing amount for each partner.
5. Using the query, create a report, sorted by last name, that lists the partner's ID, first and last names, the amount of revenue they have generated over the past year, their annual salary, and the amount of profit sharing each partner is entitled to.
6. Format the report attractively, then print one copy of it.

Visual Workshop

Create the "Emergency Contact" table shown in Figure VW-1 in a database called "Contact Sheets." Create a query to find all active employees, and then create the report shown in Figure VW-2.

FIGURE VW-1: Emergency Contact table

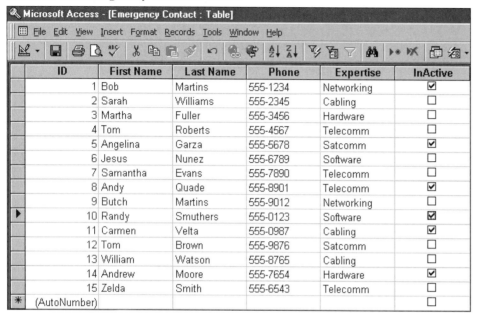

FIGURE VW-2: Emergency Contact report

Emergency Contact List

Expertise   Cabling

Last Name	First Name	ID	Phone
Watson	William	13	555-8765
Williams	Sarah	2	555-2345

Expertise   Hardware

Last Name	First Name	ID	Phone
Fuller	Martha	3	555-3456

Expertise   Networking

Last Name	First Name	ID	Phone
Martins	Butch	9	555-9012

Expertise   Satcomm

Last Name	First Name	ID	Phone
Brown	Tom	12	555-9876

Expertise   Software

Last Name	First Name	ID	Phone
Nunez	Jesus	6	555-6789

Expertise   Telecomm

Last Name	First Name	ID	Phone
Evans	Samantha	7	555-7890
Roberts	Tom	4	555-4567
Smith	Zelda	15	555-6543

Page 1 of 1

Microsoft
► Access
Projects

Personal Databases

In this unit you will create:

► Personal Gifts Database

► Family Genealogy

► Marine Circumnavigation Records

You can use Microsoft Access to track personal information of importance to you. In addition to tracking contact information on friends or business associates, you can use a database to record personal expenses, such as donations, tax information, investments, and assets, and keep important information about your personal holdings, such as a household inventory or coin and stamp collections. From these databases, you can estimate the amount of your expenses and the value of your holdings and collections and produce reports for insurance purposes. You can also track information on personal projects such as genealogical records, personal collections and inventories, athletic performances, and other types of personal accomplishments. ► In this unit you will learn how to use Access to create and work with personal databases. You will create relational and non-relational database tables with the Table Wizard and Design View, create queries with calculated fields that use simple formulas and built-in functions, and create and customize reports.

Personal Gifts Database

Each year you donate a percentage of your income to a variety of non-profit organizations. Since you work as a consultant and have a variable income, the amount that you can contribute varies from quarter to quarter and from year to year. To reach your goal of donating a percentage of your yearly income to these organizations, you decide to create a relational database to track the names and addresses of the organizations and the amount of your gifts. Since some nonprofits lobby state and federal governments, their gifts are not tax-deductible, so you will also need to track whether a gift is tax-deductible. As an aid to your financial planning, you want to create a report that shows how much you should contribute to each organization next year based on your projected income. You expect your income next year to increase by 20%.

Project Activities

Create an Organizations Table

The first database table you create will contain the names and addresses of the organizations to which you contributed this last year.

Create a Gifts Table

The second database table you create will track information on each gift to the organizations listed in the Organizations Table.

Create a Gifts Query

After building your Gifts table, you want to establish a relationship between the two tables, and then create a query that shows your contributions for the last year by quarter and that projects your expected contributions for the upcoming year.

Create a Personal Gifts Report

Next you want to create a custom report that shows your previous year's gifts, your planned gifts for next year, and a projected date for each gift you make in the next year.

When you have completed Project 1, your report will look like the one in Figure P1-1.

Personal Gifts

TaxQuarter	Organization	1997 Gift	Date	1998 Gift	Gift Date	Deductible
1						
	Gorilla Foundation	$75.00	2/7/97	$90.00	2/7/98	☑
	National Easter Seals Society	$45.00	3/21/97	$54.00	3/21/98	☑
	San Francisco SPCA Cinderella Fund	$100.00	2/28/97	$120.00	2/28/98	☑
2						
	Bird Rescue Center	$45.00	5/18/97	$54.00	5/18/98	☑
	San Francisco Ballet	$60.00	4/14/97	$72.00	4/14/98	☑
3						
	Cancer Fund of America, Inc.	$35.00	7/13/97	$42.00	7/13/98	☑
	National Child Health Foundation	$50.00	8/5/97	$60.00	8/5/98	☐
	Physicians Committee for Responsible Medicine	$25.00	6/21/97	$30.00	6/21/98	☐
	Primarily Primates, Inc.	$75.00	6/12/97	$90.00	6/12/98	☑
4						
	American Kidney Fund	$40.00	12/10/97	$48.00	12/10/98	☑
	Arthritis Research Institute of America	$45.00	11/21/97	$54.00	11/21/98	☑
	Bayshore Child Care Services	$100.00	11/21/97	$120.00	11/21/98	☑
	California Native Plant Society	$35.00	9/22/97	$42.00	9/22/98	☐
	International Eye Foundation	$50.00	10/19/97	$60.00	10/19/98	☑
	National Federation of the Blind	$55.00	10/28/97	$66.00	10/28/98	☑

Monday, February 09, 1998

PROJECT 1

PERSONAL GIFTS DATABASE

activity:

Create an Organizations Table

This table will contain the names and addresses of the organizations to which you contributed this last year. You want to create this table in Design View so that you can specify an organization code as your primary key.

steps:

1. Start Microsoft Access, then create a database named **Personal Gifts**
You decide to define the fields and properties for the first table in Design View.

2. On the Tables sheet, click **New**, double-click **Design View**, then maximize the Design View window
Next, you want to create a primary key field to store organization codes. You also want to specify a caption for the primary key field that includes a space, so that it is easier to read in Datasheet View.

3. In the first Field Name cell, type **DonorID**, press **[Enter]**, click the **Caption cell** on the General Field Properties sheet, type **Donor ID**, click the **DonorID field row selector**, then click the **Primary Key button** 🔑 on the Table Design toolbar
Access automatically uses a Text Data Type for this field and identifies it as the primary key. Now you can create the remaining fields.

4. Using Figure P1-2, enter the remaining field names and define field properties
Next you want to save and name your table.

5. Click the **Save button** 💾 on the Table Design toolbar, type **Organizations** in the Table Name box on the Save As dialog box, then click **OK**
To make data entry easier, you want to create an input mask for the Zip field.

Access 7 Users

The sample value that shows the symbols in the Mask is 98052-6399.

6. Click the **Zip field row selector**, click the **Input Mask cell** on the General Field Properties sheet, click the **Build button** 🔨 on the Table Design toolbar, click **Zip Code** in the Input Mask list box of the Input Mask Wizard dialog box, click **Next**, click **Next** to select the default input mask and placeholder character, click the **With the symbols in the mask, like this 55555-5555 option button**, click **Next**, then click **Finish**
Access creates an input mask for the Zip field. Now you are ready to enter the data for this first table.

Hint

To verify each entry that you typed, periodically double-click the border between fields to automatically adjust field widths.

7. Click the **View button** on the Table Design toolbar, then enter the data shown in Figure P1-3

8. Save and close the table

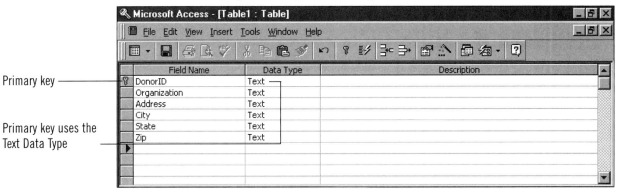

FIGURE P1-2: **Field definitions for the Organizations table**

Primary key ─────

Primary key uses the
Text Data Type ─────

FIGURE P1-3: **Data for records 1 to 15 of the Organizations table**

Donor ID ─────

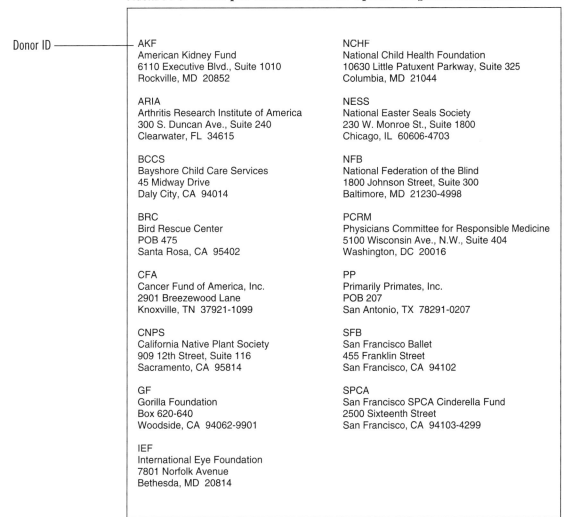

AKF
American Kidney Fund
6110 Executive Blvd., Suite 1010
Rockville, MD 20852

ARIA
Arthritis Research Institute of America
300 S. Duncan Ave., Suite 240
Clearwater, FL 34615

BCCS
Bayshore Child Care Services
45 Midway Drive
Daly City, CA 94014

BRC
Bird Rescue Center
POB 475
Santa Rosa, CA 95402

CFA
Cancer Fund of America, Inc.
2901 Breezewood Lane
Knoxville, TN 37921-1099

CNPS
California Native Plant Society
909 12th Street, Suite 116
Sacramento, CA 95814

GF
Gorilla Foundation
Box 620-640
Woodside, CA 94062-9901

IEF
International Eye Foundation
7801 Norfolk Avenue
Bethesda, MD 20814

NCHF
National Child Health Foundation
10630 Little Patuxent Parkway, Suite 325
Columbia, MD 21044

NESS
National Easter Seals Society
230 W. Monroe St., Suite 1800
Chicago, IL 60606-4703

NFB
National Federation of the Blind
1800 Johnson Street, Suite 300
Baltimore, MD 21230-4998

PCRM
Physicians Committee for Responsible Medicine
5100 Wisconsin Ave., N.W., Suite 404
Washington, DC 20016

PP
Primarily Primates, Inc.
POB 207
San Antonio, TX 78291-0207

SFB
San Francisco Ballet
455 Franklin Street
San Francisco, CA 94102

SPCA
San Francisco SPCA Cinderella Fund
2500 Sixteenth Street
San Francisco, CA 94103-4299

Clues to Use

Using input masks

Input masks simplify the data entry process for common types of data used in tables, such as social security numbers, extended zip codes, telephone numbers with the area code, and dates, all of which have specific formats. Input masks insert the proper formatting symbols, such as dashes, parentheses, and slashes, for the type of data you enter, and also guarantee that all the data in a field has the same format.

activity:

Create a Gifts Table

You also want to use Design View to define and customize the Gifts table. This table will contain the organization code as the primary key, and show the gift amount, gift date, check number, tax quarter of the gift, and whether the gift is tax-deductible.

steps:

1. On the Tables sheet, click **New**, then double-click **Design View**

   You want to create a primary key field to store organization codes and specify a caption with a space, so that it is easier to read in Datasheet View.

2. In the first Field Name cell, type **DonorID**, press **[Enter]**, click the **Caption cell** on the General Field Properties sheet, type **Donor ID**, click the **DonorID field row selector**, then click the **Primary Key button** on the Table Design toolbar

   Now you can create the remaining fields.

3. Using Figure P1-4, enter the remaining field names and specify Data Types for the fields, then save the table

   Next customize the Gift field.

4. Click the **Gift field row selector**, click the **Format cell** on the General Field Properties sheet, click the **Format list arrow**, click **Currency**, click the **Decimal Places cell**, click the **Decimal Places list arrow**, click **2**, click the **Caption cell**, then type **1997 Gift**

   You want to specify a caption with a space for the CheckNumber and TaxQuarter fields so that the column headings on your custom report also include the space.

5. Click the **CheckNumber field row selector**, click the **Caption cell** on the General Field Properties sheet, type **Check Number**, click the **TaxQuarter field row selector**, click the **Caption cell** on the General Field Properties sheet, type **Tax Quarter**

   Now you are ready to save the table definitions before you enter the data for this table.

Hint

To add a check mark to or remove a check mark from a check box, press the [Spacebar].

6. Click the **View button** on the Table Design toolbar, save the table as **Gifts**, then enter the data shown in Figure P1-5

7. Save and close the table

FIGURE P1-4: **Field definitions for the Gifts table**

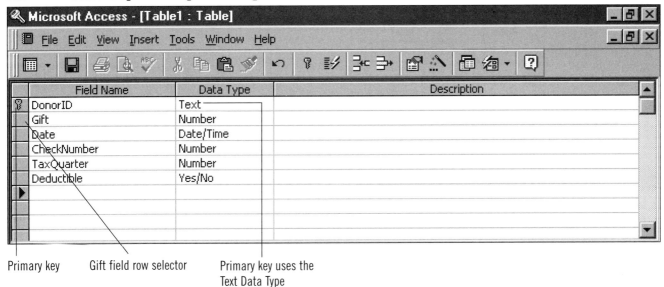

Primary key   Gift field row selector   Primary key uses the Text Data Type

FIGURE P1-5: **Data for records 1 to 15 of the Gifts table**

DonorID	1997 Gift	Date	Check Number	Tax Quarter	Deductible
AKF	$40.00	12/10/97	1285	4	☑
ARIA	$45.00	11/21/97	1271	4	☑
BCCS	$100.00	11/21/97	1270	4	☑
BRC	$45.00	5/18/97	1162	2	☑
CFA	$35.00	7/13/97	1197	3	☑
CNPS	$35.00	9/22/97	1226	4	☐
GF	$75.00	2/7/97	1117	1	☑
IEF	$50.00	10/19/97	1245	4	☑
NCHF	$50.00	8/5/97	1204	3	☐
NESS	$45.00	3/21/97	1141	1	☑
NFB	$55.00	10/28/97	1259	4	☑
PCRM	$25.00	6/21/97	1182	3	☐
PP	$75.00	6/12/97	1173	3	☑
SFB	$60.00	4/14/97	1155	2	☑
SPCA	$100.00	2/28/97	1125	1	☑
	$0.00		0	0	☐

activity:

Create a Gifts Query

Before you can create a query that shows the past year's gifts and the estimated gifts for the next year, you need to establish a relationship between the two tables. Then you can use the Query Wizard to create a select query that includes specific fields from both tables as well as a calculated field that estimates the amount that you should donate next year.

Trouble

If you do not see a Show Table dialog box, click the Show Table button [icon] on the Relationship toolbar.

steps:

1. In the Microsoft Access - [Personal Gifts: Database] window, click the **Relationships button** [icon] on the Database toolbar, and when the Show Table dialog box opens, double-click **Organizations** in the Tables list box, double-click **Gifts**, then click **Close**

   Now you can define the relationship between the two tables.

2. Drag an icon of the **DonorID field** from the Gifts field list box to the **DonorID field** in the Organizations field list box, release the mouse button, and, when the Relationships dialog box opens, click **Create**

   Access creates a one-to-one relationship between the two tables, as shown in Figure P1-6. Now you can save the relationship, close the Relationships window, and then create your query.

3. Save the relationship, then close the Relationships window

4. Click the **Queries tab**, click **New**, double-click **Simple Query Wizard**, click the **Tables/Queries list arrow**, click **Tables: Organizations** (if necessary), double-click **Organization** in the Available Fields list box, click the **Tables/Queries list arrow**, click **Tables: Gifts**, double-click **Gift** in the Available Fields list box, double-click **Date**, double-click **TaxQuarter**, double-click **Deductible**, click **Next**, click **Next** to show all detail, enter the name **Organizations Query** in the query name box (if necessary), click the **Modify the query design option button**, then click **Finish**

   Access creates a multi-table query. Now you want to add a calculated field to the query.

Access 7 Users

Click Column on the Insert menu.

5. Click the **TaxQuarter field column selector**, click **Insert** on the menu bar, click **Columns**, click in the new **Field cell** in the Design Grid, then type **1998 Gift: [Gift]*1.2** then click the **Show check box** for this field

   Now you want to format this field for currency.

6. Click in the **1998 Gift Field cell**, click the **Properties button** [icon] on the Query Design toolbar, click in the **Format box** of the General sheet of the Field Properties dialog box, click the **Format list arrow**, click **Currency**, then close the Field Properties dialog box

   Now you can run and then save the updated query.

7. Click the **Run button** [icon] on the Query Design toolbar

   Figure P1-7 shows the revised query with the 1998 estimated gift for each organization.

8. Save the query

FIGURE P1-6: Relationship between the Organizations and Gifts tables

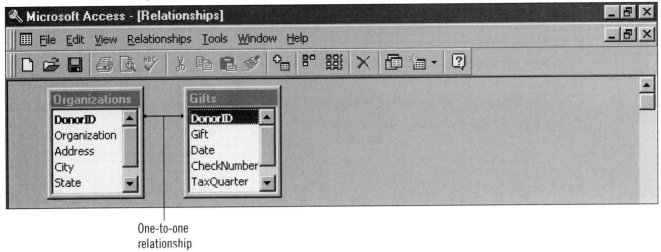

One-to-one
relationship

FIGURE P1-7: Revised query with 1998 estimated gifts

Organization	1997 Gift	Date	1998 Gift	Tax Quarter	Deduct
American Kidney Fund	$40.00	12/10/97	$48.00	4	☑
Arthritis Research Institute of America	$45.00	11/21/97	$54.00	4	☑
Bayshore Child Care Services	$100.00	11/21/97	$120.00	4	☑
Bird Rescue Center	$45.00	5/18/97	$54.00	2	☑
Cancer Fund of America, Inc.	$35.00	7/13/97	$42.00	3	☑
California Native Plant Society	$35.00	9/22/97	$42.00	4	☐
Gorilla Foundation	$75.00	2/7/97	$90.00	1	☑
International Eye Foundation	$50.00	10/19/97	$60.00	4	☑
National Child Health Foundation	$50.00	8/5/97	$60.00	3	☐
National Easter Seals Society	$45.00	3/21/97	$54.00	1	☑
National Federation of the Blind	$55.00	10/28/97	$66.00	4	☑
Physicians Committee for Responsible Medicine	$25.00	6/21/97	$30.00	3	☐
Primarily Primates, Inc.	$75.00	6/12/97	$90.00	3	☑
San Francisco Ballet	$60.00	4/14/97	$72.00	2	☑
San Francisco SPCA Cinderella Fund	$100.00	2/28/97	$120.00	1	☑

Calculated field

Clues to Use

Selecting a Column

To select a column, point to the column selector for a field in the Design Grid, and when the mouse pointer changes to ↓, click to highlight the column. You can now insert a column before the selected column, move the column, or delete the column.

activity:

Create a Personal Gifts Report

Next you want to use the Report Wizard to create a custom report that shows your previous year's gifts and your planned gifts for next year. You also realize it would be useful to include a projected date for each gift you make in the next year. Before you can prepare the report, you need to revise your query again.

steps:

1. Click the **View button** [icon] on the Query Datasheet toolbar, click the **TaxQuarter field column selector**, click **Insert** on the menu bar, click **Columns**, click the new **Field cell** in the Design grid, type **Gift Date: DateAdd("yyyy",1,[Date])** as shown in Figure P1-8, then click the **Show check box** for this field to select it

   Now you can run and then save the updated query.

2. Click the **Run button** [icon] on the Query Design toolbar, then save the revised query

   Access adds a year to the date of the 1997 gift. Now you are ready to create the report.

3. Click the **New Object button list arrow** [icon] on the Query Datasheet toolbar, click **Report**, double-click **Report Wizard**, click the **Select All Fields button** [icon], click **Next**, double-click **TaxQuarter** to group report items by this field, click **Next**, click the **1 list arrow**, click **Organization**, click **Next**, click the **Stepped option button** in the Layout area (if necessary), click **Landscape** in the Orientation area, click the **Adjust the field width so all fields fit on a page check box** (if necessary), click **Next**, click **Casual** when prompted for the style, click **Next**, type **Personal Gifts** in the report name box, click the **Preview the report option button** (if necessary), then click **Finish**

   After examining the previewed report, you decide to modify the position and size of certain fields.

4. Click **Close** on the Print Preview toolbar

   You want to center the TaxQuarter text box under the TaxQuarter report heading.

5. In the TaxQuarter Header section, click the **TaxQuarter text box**, point to the handle on the right, and when the pointer changes to ◄►, drag the handle to the ½-inch mark on the ruler

   You want to widen the Organization text box to show the full name of each organization.

6. In the Page Header section, click the **Organization label box**, press and hold **[Shift]**, click the **Organization text box** in the Detail section, point to the handle on the left, and when the pointer changes to ◄►, drag the handle to the 1-inch mark on the ruler, as shown in Figure P1-9

   You want to center the Deductible check box under the Deductible report heading.

7. In the Detail section, click the **Deductible check box** and drag it to the 8½-inch mark on the ruler

   You may need to scroll to reach the 8½-inch mark.

8. Save and print the report, then close the report and the database

FIGURE P1-8: Using the DateAdd function in the Gift Date query field

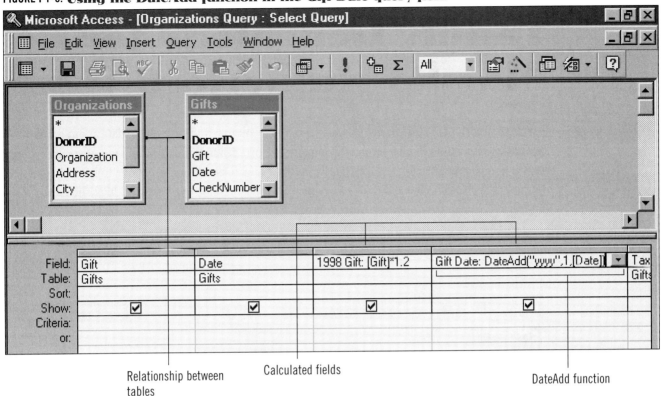

Relationship between tables

Calculated fields

DateAdd function

FIGURE P1-9: Adjusting the position of the Organization label and text box controls on the report

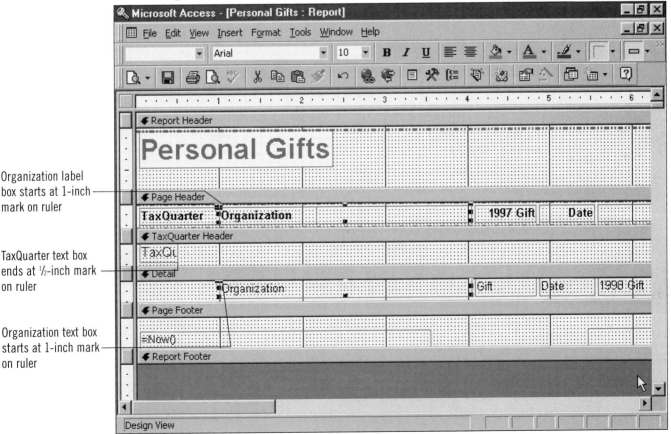

Organization label box starts at 1-inch mark on ruler

TaxQuarter text box ends at ½-inch mark on ruler

Organization text box starts at 1-inch mark on ruler

Family Genealogy for Marsha Rutherford

Marsha Rutherford, a close friend of yours, has asked you to help her organize data about her family's genealogy. She would like to record the ancestry of two generations of family members and print a report that she can distribute to key family members for review and correction. To help Marsha with her project you will **create a database, design and enter data for two related tables, filter the tables, and then create and print two custom reports.**

activities:

Design and Enter Data for Two Related Database Tables

You will create a database and define two tables: a first Generation table and a second Generation table. The first table will be used to maintain demographic data about the first generation of family members born in the United States. It will contain such data as the family member's name, when they were born, when they died, when they were married, and who their spouse was. The second table will contain data about the second generation of U.S.-born family members: when they were born, when they died, who their parents were, when they were married, and who their spouse was.

steps:

1. Create a new database based on the **Blank Database template** and name it **Rutherford's Genealogy**
Having created the database, you will now need to create the two tables you will use to maintain and manage the data for the Rutherford genealogy.

Hint
Define the ID field as the table's primary key.

2. Using **Design View**, create the table shown in Figure P2-1, then save it as **1st Generation**
Having defined the table in which you will maintain information about the first generation of U.S.-born Rutherfords, you can now enter the data for it.

3. Switch to **Datasheet View**, enter the data as shown in Figure P2-2, then close the table
Your table should resemble the one shown in Figure P2-2. You are now ready to create the second table.

Hint
Define the ID field as the table's primary key.

4. Using **Design View**, create the table shown in Figure P2-3
This table will be used to identify the descendants of the people you entered into the 1st Generation table. Your completed design should match the one shown in Figure P2-3.

5. Save the table as **2nd Generation**, switch to **Datasheet View**, then enter the data as shown in Figure P2-4
Your table should resemble the one shown in Figure P2-4.

6. Save and then close the table

FIGURE P2-1: **Design View for 1st Generation table**

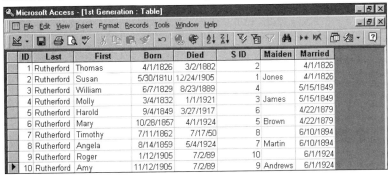

FIGURE P2-2: **Data records 1 to 10 for the 1st Generation table**

ID	Last	First	Born	Died	S ID	Maiden	Married
1	Rutherford	Thomas	4/1/1826	3/2/1882	2		4/1/1826
2	Rutherford	Susan	5/30/181U	12/24/1905	1	Jones	4/1/1826
3	Rutherford	William	6/7/1829	8/23/1889	4		5/15/1849
4	Rutherford	Molly	3/4/1832	1/1/1921	3	James	5/15/1849
5	Rutherford	Harold	9/4/1849	3/27/1917	6		4/22/1879
6	Rutherford	Mary	10/28/1857	4/1/1924	5	Brown	4/22/1879
7	Rutherford	Timothy	7/11/1862	7/17/50	8		6/10/1894
8	Rutherford	Angela	8/14/1859	5/4/1924	7	Martin	6/10/1894
9	Rutherford	Roger	1/12/1905	7/2/89	10		6/1/1924
10	Rutherford	Amy	11/12/1905	7/2/89	9	Andrews	6/1/1924

FIGURE P2-3: **Design View of 2nd Generation table**

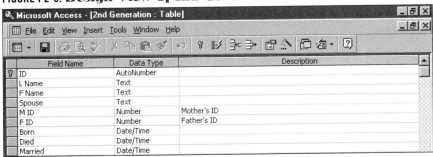

FIGURE P2-4: **Data records 1 to 10 for the 2nd Generation table**

ID	L Name	F Name	Spouse	M ID	F ID	Born	Died	Married
1	Rutherford	James		2	1	3/28/1828	6/6/1837	
2	Rutherford	William		2	1	6/7/1829	8/23/1889	
3	Burns	Anne	George	2	1	7/17/1835	6/4/1879	6/4/1866
4	Rutherford	Harold		4	3	9/4/1849	3/27/1917	
5	Rutherford	Timothy		4	3	7/11/1862	7/17/1950	
6	Rutherford	Mary		6	5	10/3/1880	6/8/1971	
7	Rutherford	Julial		6	5	10/3/1880	10/12/1897	
8	Rutherford	Marian		8	7	1/13/1905	10/12/1970	
9	Rutherford	Roger		8	7	11/12/1905	3/9/1924	
10	Rutherford	Marsha		10	9	7/2/1929		

Clues to Use

Working with dates

Access displays the full year for dates prior to 1930, the last two digits of the year for dates from 1930 to 2029, and the full year for dates after 2029. If you want to enter four-digit years after 1930, you need to change the default input mask from 99/99/00 to 99/99/0000 so that Access allows you to enter the full year with four digits. First, select the date field in Design View, select the Input Mask box on the General Field Properties sheet, click the Build button , select the Short Date format (for example, 6/20/91), and at the next step, click the Input Mask text box and type two additional zeroes at the end of the default input mask.

FAMILY GENEALOGY FOR MARSHA RUTHERFORD

activity:

Creating Relationships and Querying the Data

Marsha has asked you to create a report showing the parents and spouses of the second generation of U.S.-born family members. Before you can prepare this report it will be necessary for you to establish relationships between the 1st Generation and 2nd Generation tables, then query the data.

Hint

To create a query that displays information about both parents you need to open the first Generation table twice, because each second Generation record accesses more than one record from the first Generation table.

Hint

You can move the table field list box by clicking on the box's title bar and dragging it to its new location.

Hint

You can establish links while in the Relationships window by dragging a field name from one table field list to the corresponding field name in another table field list.

Time To
✓ **Close**

steps:

1. Click the **Relationships button** [icon] on the Database toolbar, add the **2nd Generation table**, then add the **1st Generation table** twice

   Access displays three field list boxes: the 2nd Generation table list box, the 1st Generation table list box, and the 1st Generation_1 table list box. In order to gain a better view of the relationships you will establish between the parent's and children's tables, you can reposition and resize these boxes.

2. Position the 1st Generation and 2nd Generation table field lists as shown in Figure P2-5

   Notice that the key fields in each table list box are in bold format. Having added the necessary table lists to the relationship window, you can now establish links between your tables.

3. Link the father's ID field, **F ID**, from the 2nd Generation table list box to the **ID field** of the 1st Generation table list box, then link the mother's ID field, **M ID**, from the 2nd Generation table list box to the **ID** field of the 1st Generation table list box

   As you establish links between your tables, Access displays join lines that indicate linked fields between tables.

4. Close the Relationships window saving the relationships when asked, then from the Queries tab of the Database window, create a new query using **Design View**

5. From the Show Table dialog box, add the **1st Generation table**, the **2nd Generation table**, then add the **1st Generation table** again

6. Remove the link from **2nd Generation table's F ID** field to the **1st Generation table's ID** field, then create a link from the **2nd Generation table's F ID** field to the **1st Generation_1 table's ID** field

   Relationships can be deleted by clicking on the join line representing the link and then pressing the Delete key. You can now select the fields you need to display.

7. From the 2nd Generation table, add the fields **F Name**, **L Name**, and **Spouse** to the Query table; from the 1st Generation table, add the fields **First** and **Last**; then from the 1st Generation table_1 add **First** and **Last**

   Your screen should match the one shown in Figure P2-6.

8. Save the query as **US Rutherfords** then click the **Run button** [icon] on the Query Datasheet toolbar

   The results of your query should match those shown in Figure P2-7.

FIGURE P2-5: **Table relationships**

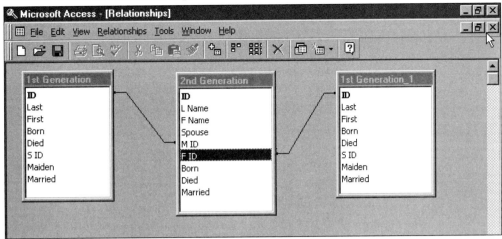

FIGURE P2-6: **US Rutherfords query in Design View**

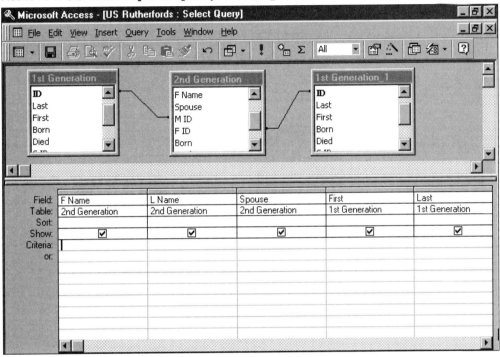

FIGURE P2-7: **US Rutherfords query in Datasheet View**

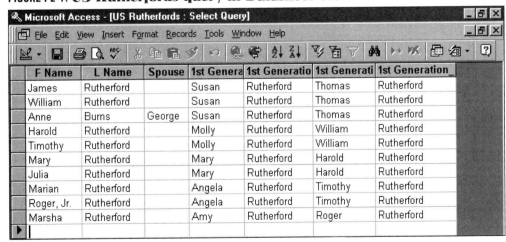

FAMILY GENEALOGY FOR MARSHA RUTHERFORD

activity:

Create a Custom Report

Marsha Rutherford would like you to create a report of second Generation family members that identifies who their spouse and parents were. To produce this custom report you will use the US Rutherfords' query to create a custom report.

steps:

1. From the Reports tab, create a new report, then select the **US Rutherfords** query and **Design View** from the New Report dialog box

Having created a new report, you can now begin to develop the report layout. For this report you will need to display the Report Header section of the report design grid and add a report title to this section.

2. Click **View** on the menu bar, click **Report Header/Footer**, then add the report header **2nd Generation US Rutherfords** using a **bold**, *italic*, **18 point**, **Times New Roman** font

You can now add the report field label in the Page Header section. These labels will appear at the top of each report page.

3. In the Page Header section, add the labels **Name**, **Spouse**, **Mother**, and **Father** using a **bold**, *italic*, **14 point**, **Times New Roman** font, then add the horizontal line using the **Line button** ◥ on the Toolbox toolbar

Your screen should resemble the one shown in Figure P2-8. You can now enter the report detail. This detail will display the required information for each record selected with the database query you previously created.

4. If necessary, click the **Field List button** 🗐 on the Report Design toolbar to display a list box of available fields

5. In the Detail section, add the field **F Name** by dragging the field name from the list box onto the detail design grid, then delete the standard field label automatically created by the dragging

6. Add the remaining fields, as shown in Figure P2-8, from the list box to the Detail design area, deleting the standard field labels as you proceed, then format all detail fields as **12 point**, **Times New Roman**

Now that you have added all the necessary data elements to the report, you can now define the sort order for the report.

7. Click the **Sorting and Grouping button** 〔≡ on the Report Design toolbar, and sort the report by the children's last name, **L Name**, then by the children's first name, **F Name**

It is a good idea to add a report object that lets the reader know which page they are viewing and how many pages are contained in the report. You can place this information in the Page Footer of the report.

8. Click **Insert** on the Menu bar, click **Page Numbers**, click **Page N of M**, click **Bottom of Page [Footer]**, select **Center** alignment, then click **OK**

9. Modify the report layout as necessary so that it resembles the report shown in Figure P2-8, then print it

Hint

As you add field objects to the report design grid, Access creates a label of the field name for each data field you add to the report. While these labels look like their corresponding data fields, they are identified as labels in the Object list box on the Formatting toolbar.

Time To

✓ **Save**

✓ **Close**

FIGURE P2-8: 2nd Generation US Rutherfords report in Design View

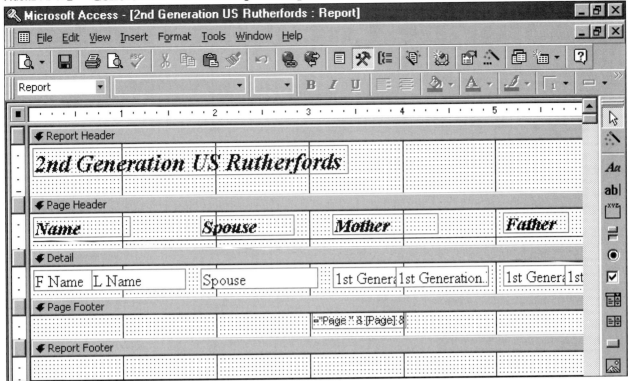

FIGURE P2-9: 2nd Generation US Rutherfords report

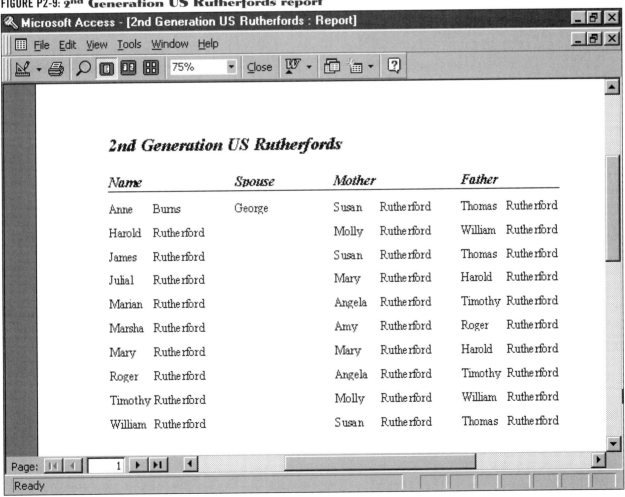

OVERVIEW

Marine Circumnavigation Records

As an avid sailor, it has always been your dream to get into the record books by single-handedly circumnavigating the globe in a sailboat. You want to accomplish this in a way that no other human has before. In researching this ambitious project, you have learned that for your trip to be accepted as a true circumnavigation, you must pass through two antipodal points that are at least 12,429 stature miles apart. You have also gathered a list of data regarding past circumnavigation accomplishments and would like to compile this list into usable information. To do so, you will **design and input a database table, query the table,** and then **create a report**.

activities:

Create the Database, Queries, and Report

steps:

1. Create a database called **Circumnavigations**, then create a table named **Records** as shown in Figure P3-1

2. Enter the data as shown in Figure P3-2

Your table should match the one shown in Figure P3-2. After reviewing your entries, you have noticed some errors that you need to correct.

3. Locate and change the vessel named **Victoria** to **Vittoria**, the sailor named **Albert Cowan** to **Albert Gowan**, and the **End Date 5/10/1969** to **5/10/1960**

4. Using **Simple Query Wizard**, create a query named **Solos Records Query** that shows all fields from the Records table except **ID** and displays only those records whose Category field contains the word **solo**

5. Modify the query to sort in ascending order by **End Date**

6. Save and close the query

7. Using **Report Wizard**, create a custom report named **Solo Records Report** as shown in Figure P3-3, using the Solo Records query, do not group or sort the report, use a Tabular Layout, a Landscaped orientation, adjust the field widths so all fields fit on a page, and a corporate style

Hint

You can use the asterisk (*) wildcard character to match any number or character. The asterisk wildcard can be used as the first or last character in the character string you are searching.

Time To

✓ **Save**

✓ **Close**

Clues to Use

Using wildcards

You can use wildcards to search for partial or matching values. The asterisk (*) wildcard can be used to match any number of characters and can be used as the last or first characters in a character(s) string. For example, wh* would find what, while, and why; *on* would find on, sony, only and wonder; and *ee would find see, knee, and glee.

FIGURE P3-1: Design View of Records table

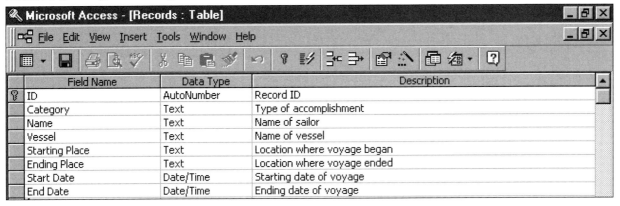

Field Name	Data Type	Description
ID	AutoNumber	Record ID
Category	Text	Type of accomplishment
Name	Text	Name of sailor
Vessel	Text	Name of vessel
Starting Place	Text	Location where voyage began
Ending Place	Text	Location where voyage ended
Start Date	Date/Time	Starting date of voyage
End Date	Date/Time	Ending date of voyage

FIGURE P3-2: Data records 1 to 12 or the Records table

ID	Category	Name	Vessel	Starting Place	Ending Place	Start Date	End Date
1	Earliest	Juan Sebastian	Victoria	Seville, Spain	San Lucar, Spain	9/20/1519	9/6/1521
2	Earliest Woman	Bare	Etoile	St. Malo, France	St. Malo, France	7/12/1766	10/3/1769
3	Earliest Yacht	Lord/Lady Brassey	Sunbeam	Isle of Wight, England	Isle of Wight, England	4/25/1876	7/10/1877
4	Earliest Solo	Jashua Slocum	Spray	Newport, USA	Newport, USA	4/24/1895	7/3/1898
5	Earliest Motor	Albert Cowen	Speedjacks	New York, USA	New York, USA	3/10/1921	5/14/1922
6	Earliest Woman Solo	Krystyna Chojnowska	Mazurek	Las Palmas, USA	Tied Knot, USA	3/28/1976	3/21/1978
7	Smallest Boat	Hiroshi Aoki	Ahdori II	Osaka, Japan	Osaka, Japan	6/12/1972	7/29/1974
8	Earliest Submarine	Edward Beach	USS Triton	New London, USA	New London, USA	2/16/1960	5/10/1969
9	Fastest Solo	Alain Colas	Manureva	St. Malo, France	St. Malo, France	9/28/1993	3/29/1994
10	Fastest	Mike Gill	Great Britain II	Thames, England	Thames, England	8/31/1975	10/9/1975
11	Fastest Solo	Kenichi Horie	Mermaid III	Osaka, Japan	Osaka, Japan	8/1/1973	5/5/1974
12	Earliest Non-stop Solo	Robin Knox	Suhaili	Falmouth, England	Falmouth, England	6/14/1968	4/22/1969

FIGURE P3-3: Solo Records report

Solo Records Report

Category	Name	Vessel	Starting Place/Date		Ending Place/Date	
Earliest Solo	Jashua Slocum	Spray	Newport, USA	4/24/1895	Newport, USA	7/3/1898
Earliest Woman Solo	Krystyna Chojnowsk	Mazurek	Las Palmas, USA	3/28/1976	Tied Knot, USA	3/21/1978
Fastest Solo	Alain Colas	Manureva	St. Malo, France	9/28/1993	St. Malo, France	3/29/1994
Fastest Solo	Kenichi Horie	Mermaid III	Osaka, Japan	8/1/1973	Osaka, Japan	5/5/1974
Earliest Non-stop Solo	Robin Knox	Suhaili	Falmouth, England	6/14/1968	Falmouth, England	4/22/1969

Independent Challenges

INDEPENDENT CHALLENGE 1

Each year you itemize deductions on your federal and state income tax forms. To simplify this tax for the next tax year, you want to create a relational database that tracks Schedule A deductions. You also want to be able to estimate the amount of those same expenses for the following year so that you can better plan your budget. In one table, you want to include information on each expense; in the other table, you want to identify the expense category based on the Schedule A line number. After examining Schedule A, you realize that all your expense deductions fall in the following categories:

Line 1	Medical and Dental Expenses	Line 10	Home Mortgage Interest
Line 5	State and Local Income Taxes	Line 15	Gifts by Check and Cash
Line 6	Real Estate Taxes	Line 20	Unreimbursed Employee Expenses
Line 7	Personal Property Taxes	Line 21	Tax Preparation Fees

After you build the two tables, you want to record your expenses for the first quarter of this year, add calculated fields for estimating next year's expenses, and then produce an expense report.

1. Using the following worksheet, identify the tables, fields, and table relationships you need for this database:

Tables	Fields	Primary Key	Linking fields

2. Create a relational database called "Schedule A Deductions" that contains at least 12 different expenses incurred during the first quarter of the year (from January through March). For example, you might include costs for a physical exam, a dental cleaning, a prescription, union dues, a computer show, and tax preparation, as well as estimated taxes and gifts to two or three charities.

3. Create a query that includes information on all tax deductible expenses, add a calculated field that estimates an 8% increase in each of the expenses for next year, and add another calculated field that calculates a date for each expense that is one year in advance of the current date.

4. Create, format, and print a report that lists tax deductible expenses by type of expense, that sorts the expenses by date, and that includes the estimated date and amount of each expense for the following tax year.

INDEPENDENT CHALLENGE 2

You are planning a costume party and want to use Access to manage your preparations. Create a relational database that contains a table listing the names, addresses, and telephone numbers of your guests. When you call your friends, you want to suggest a costume for them to wear. You plan to use the contact list for future parties and events, so you need to create a separate table for the costume information. Your second table will contain a list of period costumes, such as Clown, 60's, New Age, Renaissance, and Medieval, that are available from the local costume store. After you build the database, you want to create a query that includes information from both tables, and then produce a report that lists the names, telephone numbers, and recommended costumes of those you want to invite. As you call each person, you want to record whether the person plans to rent the costume or create their own.

1. Using the following worksheet, identify the tables, fields, and table relationships you need for this database:

Tables	Fields	Primary Key	Linking fields

2. Create a relational database called Costume Party with one table that contains information on your friends and another that lists available costumes.
3. Create a Costumes query that includes the information you need to call each person and the type of costume you want them to rent.
4. Create, format, and print a report that lists the contact information for each guest, each person's recommended costume, and a column for noting whether each person will rent or create the costume.

INDEPENDENT CHALLENGE 3

As an avid movie buff and video collector, you would like to create a database that contains information about your favorite actors and films. You have decided to create two tables. The first table will contain information about your videos and will be linked to the second table containing information about the leading men and women. The first table might include such data as the title, the year it was released, the IDs of each of the leading men and women, the running time, and the genre (such as film noir, action, or western). The second table might include the leading person's name and birth date. Later on, you plan to create tables containing information on favorite directors and producers.

1. Create a database called "My Videos."
2. Create a table named "Leading People" to contain the data regarding your favorite actors, and then enter the necessary records into it.
3. Create a table named "Titles" to maintain the data regarding the videos, and then add 10 records to it.
4. Create a report, sorted by video title, that lists the name of the film, the year it was released, and the name of the primary star.

Your home insurer, Northeast Insurance Company, has asked you to provide them with a listing of all your household items that you would like insured against theft or damage. They would like you to supply them with such information as a brief description of the item, its serial number (if one exists), the original purchase date and price of the item, and its estimated replacement cost. Because Northeast would like you to provide them with this list annually, you have decided to maintain this data in an Access table.

1. Create a database called "Northeast Inventory."
2. Create a table called "Personal Items."
3. Develop and enter data for between 10 and 15 insurable household items.
4. Create and print a report, sorted by item, that lists the information requested by Northeast Insurance.

Visual Workshop

Using Figure VW-1, create a database called "Waterfalls of the World." Then create a query to find all waterfalls that have a drop of over 2000 feet, sort the Drop in Feet field in descending order, and then, using Design View, create the report shown in Figure VW-2.

FIGURE VW-1: Waterfalls table

Fall ID	Name	Drop in Feet	Location	Country
1	Angel Falls	3212	Carrao River	Venezuela
2	Glass Fall	3110	Iguazi	Brazil
3	Yosemite	2425	California	United States
4	Sutherland Falls	1904	River Arthur	New Zealand
5	King George VI	1600	Utshi	Guyana
6	Gavarnie	1384	Gave de Pau	France
7	Tugela	3110	Natal	South Africa
8	Takkakaw	1248	Yoho River, B.C.	Canada
9	Serio	1033	Lombardy	Italy
10	Utigardsfossen	2625	Utigards	Norway
11	Wollomombi	1580	N.S.W.	Australia
12	Lofoi	1259	Congo	Zaire
13	Staubbach	978	Bernese	Switzerland
14	Guaira	374	Alto Parana River	Paraguay

FIGURE VW-2: Waterfall report

Waterfalls of the World (2000' and Over)

Drop in Feet: 2425

Name	Location	Country
Yosemite	California	United States

Drop in Feet: 2625

Name	Location	Country
Utigardsfossen	Utigards	Norway

Drop in Feet: 3110

Name	Location	Country
Tugela	Natal	South Africa
Glass Fall	Iguazi	Brazil

Drop in Feet: 3212

Name	Location	Country
Angel Falls	Carrao River	Venezuela

Microsoft
► Access
Projects

General Business Databases

In This Unit You Will Create:

 ► **Cuisine Database**

 ► **Power Plant Database**

 ► **Book List**

Although Microsoft Access is invaluable to large businesses that track large quantities of information, Access is also ideal for small businesses and their specialized needs. You can use Access to create and work with many different types of databases used by businesses and organizations, such as databases that track information on services, products, transactions, accounts payable, accounts receivable, and listings. From these databases, you can then design special types of reports, such as a restaurant menu, a list of realty properties, inventories, and delinquent client accounts. You can evaluate the effects of increasing or decreasing product prices and services, as well as increased operating expenses. ► In this unit you will learn how to use Access to create and work with general business databases. You will create relational and non-relational database tables, create queries with calculated fields that use simple formulas and built-in functions, create queries and reports with summary data, and design special types of reports.

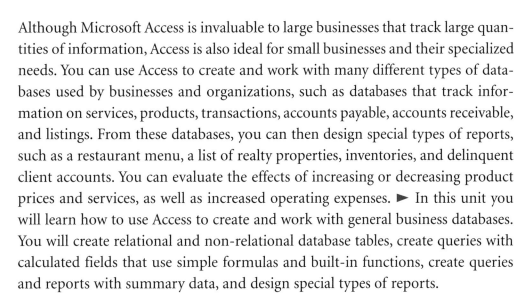

Tandoori Delicacies Database

You and your family operate a restaurant called Tandoori Delicacies, which specializes in Indian vegetarian dishes, accompaniments, breads, and desserts. You want to create a database that contains a list of the items on your current menu, and then you want to create a new restaurant menu. In response to increased operating costs, you also want to query the database and decide how best to increase the cost of your dishes.

Project Activities

Create a Cuisine Table

You will create a relational database for Tandoori Delicacies. The first table will contain information on Indian cuisine served at this restaurant.

Create a Menu Table

The second database table will contain information on the four types of cuisine on the restaurant's menu. As you create this table, you will define a one-to-many relationship with the first table. By establishing this relationship, you will be able to prepare a restaurant menu that draws on information from both tables.

Create a Restaurant Menu

You will create a restaurant menu that lists individual dishes by category, since this is how most menus are organized. Then you will customize the restaurant menu to make it look even more professional and eye-catching.

Create a Price Query

You will create a query with calculated fields that looks at two possible types of price increases for the restaurant.

When you have completed Project 1, your restaurant menu will appear similar to the one in Figure P1-1.

Tandoori Delicacies

Menu Category	Indian Cuisine	English Name	Price
Accompaniments			
	Adrak Chatni	Ginger Chutney	$3.25
	Raita	Yogurt Salad	$4.75
	Sambal	Chilled Spicy Vegetable Salad	$4.50
	Tamatar Chatni	Tomato Chutney	$3.00
Vegetarian Cuisine			
	Alu Makhala	Jumping Potatoes	$7.95
	Channa Dhal	Curried Chickpeas	$8.55
	Ekuri	Scrambled Eggs with Chili	$6.45
	Khichri	Rice with Lentils	$7.25
	Pakoras	Vegetable Fritters	$7.50
	Sabzi Kari	Vegetable Curry	$6.75
	Sambar	Lentils Cooked with Spices	$8.25
	Vendai Kai Kari	Curried Okra	$6.65
	Wengyachen Bharit	Curried Aubergines	$7.75
Breads			
	Paratha	Fried Wholewheat Bread	$3.75
	Puris	Deep-Fried Bread	$3.50
Desserts			
	Gulab Jamun	Deep-Fried Dough Balls	$4.95
	Halva	Semolina Fudge	$4.50
	Kulfi	Mango Ice Cream	$4.25

activity:

Create a Cuisine Table

In your Tandoori Delicacies database, you want to create a Cuisine table that contains information on the different types of Indian cuisine served at your restaurant.

steps:

1. Start Access, then create a database named **Tandoori Delicacies** on the disk where you are storing your files for this book

   You will use Design View to define the fields and properties for the Cuisine table.

2. On the Tables tab, click **New**, double-click **Design View** in the New Table dialog box, then maximize the Design View window

   Next you want to create a Menu ID field that will serve as the primary key for the database table.

3. In the first Field Name cell, type **MenuID**, press **[Enter]**, click the **Data Type list arrow** for the MenuID field, then click **AutoNumber**

   Now you want to define the MenuID field as the primary key and change the caption.

4. Click the **Primary Key button** 🔑 on the Table Design toolbar, click in the Caption cell on the General Field Properties sheet for the MenuID field, then type **Menu ID**

   Now you can create the remaining fields. You will use captions that include spaces so that field names are easier to read in Datasheet View and also appear in a format you would expect on a report.

5. Using Figure P1-2 as a guideline, enter the remaining field names, define the Data Type for each field, and specify field Captions (not field Descriptions)

   Now you are ready to enter the data for this first table.

Access 7 Users

Click the Table View button 📝 ▾ on the Design View toolbar to switch to Datasheet View.

6. Click the **View button** ▦ ▾ on the Table Design toolbar, and when prompted, click **Yes** to save the table, type **Cuisine** in the Save As dialog box, click **OK**, then enter the data shown in Figure P1-3

7. Save and close the table

FIGURE P1-2: **Fields and field properties of the Cuisine table**

Field	Data Type	Caption
MenuID	AutoNumber	Menu ID
IndianCuisine	Text	Indian Cuisine
EnglishName	Text	English Name
Price	Currency	
CategoryID	Number	Category ID

FIGURE P1-3: **Data for records 1 to 18 of the Cuisine table**

Microsoft Access - [Cuisine : Table]

File Edit View Insert Format Records Tools Window Help

Menu ID	Indian Cuisine	English Name	Price	Category ID
1	Adrak Chatni	Ginger Chutney	$3.25	1
2	Alu Makhala	Jumping Potatoes	$7.95	2
3	Channa Dhal	Curried Chickpeas	$8.55	2
4	Ekuri	Scrambled Eggs with Chili	$6.45	2
5	Gulab Jamun	Deep-Fried Dough Balls	$4.95	4
6	Halva	Semolina Fudge	$4.50	4
7	Khichri	Rice with Lentils	$7.25	2
8	Kulfi	Mango Ice Cream	$4.25	4
9	Pakoras	Vegetable Fritters	$7.50	2
10	Paratha	Fried Wholewheat Bread	$3.75	3
11	Puris	Deep-Fried Bread	$3.50	3
12	Raita	Yogurt Salad	$4.75	1
13	Sabzi Kari	Vegetable Curry	$6.75	2
14	Sambal	Chilled Spicy Vegetable Salad	$4.50	1
15	Sambar	Lentils Cooked with Spices	$8.25	2
16	Tamatar Chatni	Tomato Chutney	$3.00	1
17	Vendai Kai Kari	Curried Okra	$6.65	2
18	Wengyachen Bharit	Curried Aubergines	$7.75	2
* oNumber)			$0.00	0

Record: 1 of 18

Datasheet View

activity:

Create a Menu Table

You also want to use Design View to define and customize the Menu table. This database table will contain information on the four types of cuisine on the restaurant's menu. As you create this table, you will define a one-to-many relationship with the Cuisine table.

steps:

1. On the Tables tab, click **New**, then double-click **Design View** in the New Table dialog box, type **CategoryID** in the first Field Name cell, press **[Enter]**, click the **Data Type list arrow** for the CategoryID field, then click **AutoNumber**

Now you want to define the CategoryID field as the primary key. You also want to change its caption so that it matches what you used in the Cuisine table and is easy to read in Datasheet View.

2. Click the **Primary Key button** 🔑 on the Table Design toolbar, click in the Caption cell on the General Field Properties sheet for the CategoryID field, then type **Category ID**

Now you can define the field that identifies the type of menu item.

3. In the second Field Name cell, type **MenuCategory** and press **[Enter]**, click the **Data Type list arrow** for this field and click **Text**, click in the Caption cell on the General Field Properties sheet for this field, then type **Menu Category**

Now you are ready to switch to Datasheet View, save the table definitions, and enter data for the table.

4. Click the **View button** ⊞▾ on the Table Design toolbar, when prompted, click **Yes** to save the table, type **Menu** in the Save As dialog box, click **OK**, then enter the data shown in Figure P1-4

After you save and close the table, you want to define the relationship between the Cuisine and Menu tables.

5. Save and close the table

Trouble

If you do not see a Show Table dialog box, click the Show Table button ⊞ on the Relationships toolbar.

6. Click the **Relationships button** 🔗 on the Database toolbar, then, using Figure P1-5 as a guide-line, create a one-to-many relationship between the Cuisine and Menu tables

7. Save the relationship, then close the Relationships window

FIGURE P1-4: **Data for records 1 to 4 of the Menu table**

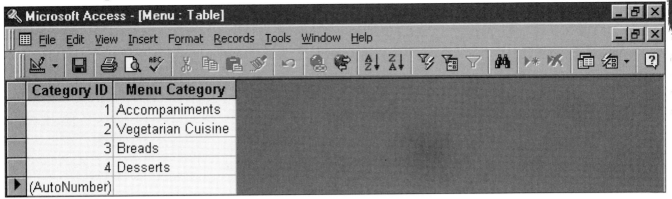

FIGURE P1-5: **Relationship between the Cuisine and Menu tables**

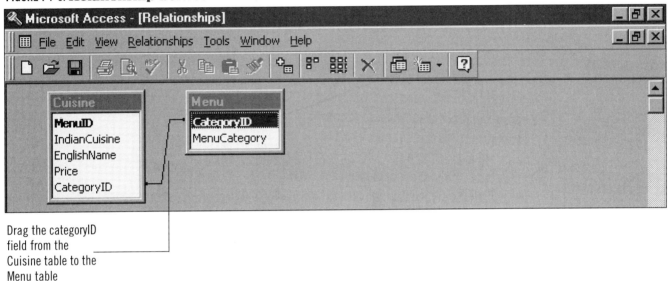

Drag the categoryID
field from the
Cuisine table to the
Menu table

Clues to Use

Creating relationships

To create a relationship, click the Relationships button 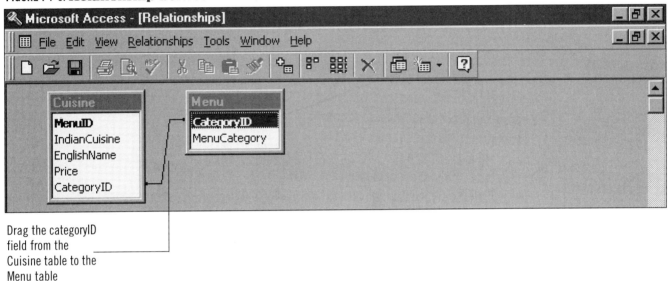 *on the Database toolbar, and when the Show Table dialog box opens, add the tables to the Relationships window, close the Show Table dialog box, drag an icon of a field from one table to the corresponding field in the other table, and then verify the type of relationship you want to create.*

activity:

Create a Restaurant Menu

You will use Report Wizard to create a restaurant menu that lists individual dishes by category. Then you will format the restaurant menu.

steps:

1. Open the **Report Wizard**, and when prompted for the table fields, click the **Tables/Queries list arrow**, click **Table: Menu**, double-click **MenuCategory** in the Available Fields list box, click the **Tables/Queries list arrow**, click **Table: Cuisine**, double-click **IndianCuisine** in the Available Fields list box, double-click **EnglishName**, double-click **Price**, then click **Next**

You want to view data by menu category, list the cuisine in alphabetical order by name, and choose the report layout and style.

2. Click **by Menu** (if necessary), then click **Next**, and when prompted for any additional grouping levels, click **Next**; when prompted about sorting options, click the **1 list arrow**, click **IndianCuisine**, and click **Next**; click **Next** to accept the default page layout settings; click **Soft Gray** when prompted for the style, click **Next**; type **Tandoori Delicacies** in the report name box, then click **Finish** to view a preview of the report

After examining the previewed report, you decide to make changes to the report format so that it appears more like a restaurant menu.

Access 7 Users

The toolbar with the Bold and Italic buttons is called the Formatting (Form/Report Design) toolbar.

3. Click **Close** on the Print Preview toolbar; using Figure P1-6 as a guideline, click the **MenuCategory text box** in the CategoryID Header section, click the **Bold button** B and the **Italic button** I on the Formatting (Form/Report) toolbar, click the **Properties button** on the Report Design toolbar, click the Format tab in the Text Box dialog box (if necessary), scroll down and click the **Border Style list arrow**, click **Transparent**, then close the Text Box: MenuCategory dialog box

You also decide to apply bold formatting to the name of the Indian cuisine and remove the page footer.

4. Click the **IndianCuisine text box** in the Detail section, click the **Bold button** B on the Formatting (Form/Report toolbar), click the **text box** with the Now() function in the Page Footer section, press and hold **[Shift]**, click the **text box** with the page numbering options, then press **[Delete]**

5. Preview and then print the report, then save and close the report

FIGURE P1-6: **Changing the design of the report**

Boldface, italicized text box with transparent border

Assign bold attribute to this text box

Delete these controls

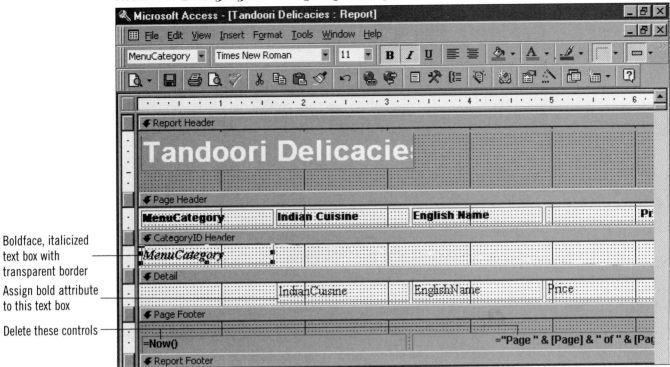

Clues to Use

Formatting a report

You can format reports in Report Design View by using options on the Formatting or Toolbox toolbars and by changing the properties of report sections or elements. Using the toolbars, you can add controls, such as label and text boxes and lines, and enhance those controls. If you select the report selector (a small box at the intersection of the rulers), you can modify properties of the entire report. If you select a section selector (the small box to the left of a section bar), you can modify properties of just that section. If you select a report control or element, you can modify properties of that control or element. If you select a property and then press the F1 key, Access will display context-sensitive help on just that property.

activity:

Create a Price Query

Since your operating costs are rising, you realize you will need to increase your prices in the near future. To assist you in choosing the best way to make this change, you want to use the Simple Query Wizard to create a select query that shows two possible approaches for price increases.

Access 7 Users

If you are using Access 7.0, you click the Query View button on the Query Datasheet toolbar.

Trouble?

If Access informs you that there is a problem with the expression, click OK, open Expression Builder, correct the problem, then click OK to save your changes.

steps:

1. Click the **Queries tab**, click **New**, double-click **Simple Query Wizard**, click the **Tables/Queries list arrow** and click **Table: Cuisine** (if necessary), double-click **IndianCuisine** in the Available Fields list box, double-click **EnglishName**, double-click **Price**, click **Next**, click **Next** to show all detail, type **Price Increases** in the query name text box, click the **Open the query to view information option button** (if necessary), then click **Finish**

   For the first possible type of price increase, you want to add a field that calculates a 15% increase in all items.

2. Click the **View button** 📇 ▾ on the Query Datasheet toolbar to switch to Design View, click in the next available Field cell in the Design grid, type **Percent Increase: [Price]*1.15**

   For the second possible type of price increase, you want to use the IIf function to increase each vegetarian dish by $1.25.

3. Click in the next available Field cell in the Design grid, click the **Build button** 📇 on the Query Design toolbar, and in the Expression Box, type **Flat Increase:** as the field name; then, using Figure P1-7 as a guideline, enter an IIf function that calculates a $1.25 increase for the vegetarian cuisine and no increase for the other dishes

   Now you want to view the new pricing options.

4. Click the **Run button** ❗ on the Query Design toolbar

   Access produces a query, but you still need to format the Percent Increase field for currency.

5. Click the **View button** 📇 ▾ on the Query Datasheet toolbar, click the **Percent Increase field**, click the **Properties button** 📇 on the Query Design toolbar, click the **Format list arrow**, click **Currency**, click in the **Decimal Places list box**, click the **Decimal Places list arrow**, click **2**, close the Field Properties dialog box, then run the query again

   Figure P1-8 shows the final query with the formatted calculated fields.

6. Print one copy of the query, then save and close it

FIGURE P1-7: Completed IIf function for the Flat Increase calculated field

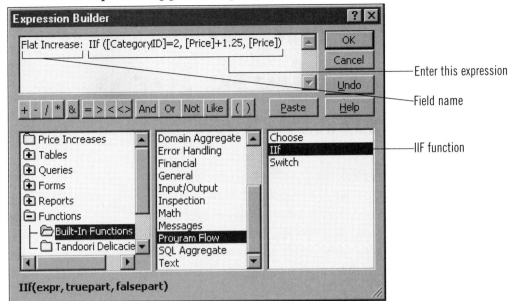

Enter this expression
Field name
IIF function

FIGURE P1-8: Price Increases query

Calculated fields

Indian Cuisine	English Name	Price	Percent Increase	Flat Increase
Adrak Chatni	Ginger Chutney	$3.25	$3.74	$3.25
Alu Makhala	Jumping Potatoes	$7.95	$9.14	$9.20
Channa Dhal	Curried Chick-Peas	$8.55	$9.83	$9.80
Ekuri	Scrambled Eggs with Chili	$6.45	$7.42	$7.70
Gulab Jamun	Deep-Fried Dough Balls	$4.95	$5.69	$4.95
Halva	Semonlina Fudge	$4.50	$5.17	$4.50
Khichri	Rice with Lentils	$7.25	$8.34	$8.50
Kulfi	Mango Ice Cream	$4.25	$4.89	$4.25
Pakoras	Vegetable Fritters	$7.50	$8.63	$8.75
Paratha	Fried Wholewheat Bread	$3.75	$4.31	$3.75
Puris	Deep-Fried Bread	$3.50	$4.02	$3.50
Raita	Yogurt Salad	$4.75	$5.46	$4.75
Sabzi Kari	Vegetable Curry	$6.75	$7.76	$8.00
Sambal	Chilled Spicy Vegetable Salad	$4.50	$5.17	$4.50
Sambar	Lentils Cooked with Spices	$8.25	$9.49	$9.50
Tamatar Chatni	Tomato Chutney	$3.00	$3.45	$3.00
Vendai Kai Kari	Curried Okra	$6.65	$7.65	$7.90
Wengyachen Bharit	Curried Aubergines	$7.75	$8.91	$9.00
*		$0.00		

Record: 1 of 18

Datasheet View

Clues to Use

Locating and specifying arguments for the IIf function

To locate the IIf function, double-click the Functions folder in the Expression Elements list box on the left, click the Built-In Functions folder, click Program Flow in the Categories list box in the center, then double-click IIf in the Functions list box on the right, click <<Expr>>, press [Delete], click <<expr>>, type your condition, click <<truepart>>, type a formula or value to use if the condition is true, click <<falsepart>>, type a formula or value to use if the condition is false, then click OK.

Hydroelectric Generating Plants database for a local Orators Group

You have enrolled in a local Orators group to improve your public speaking skills. At the last meeting you attended, members were assigned a topic about which to give an informative speech. Your topic is *Hydroelectric Power*. As part of your preparation, you have researched your topic using the Internet and have come across various reports and articles specific to your topic. To better organize your thoughts, you have decided to maintain this information using Microsoft Access. To do so, you will **create a database table, modify its structure, enter and edit records, create a custom query,** and then **create a custom report**.

activities:

Create the Database Tables and Enter Data

To organize the information you have collected, you will create a table named Hydroelectric Plants table that properly identifies the individual pieces of information you will include in your database. You will then modify the table structure and enter the data you have found during your research.

steps:

1. Start Access, then create a new database based on the **Blank Database template**, name the database **Hydroelectric**, then save it to the disk on which you are saving your files for this book
You will now create the power plants table.

2. On the **Tables tab** click **New**, click **Design View**, click **OK**, then enter the following field names: **Plant ID**, **Plant Name**, **Location**, **River**, **Kilowatts**, and **Staff**
Access automatically assigns Text as the data type for all fields. Now you need to change some of the field types and designate a Primary Key field.

3. Click the **Data Type cell** for the Plant ID field, click the **Data Type list arrow**, click **AutoNumber**, press **Tab**, then type **Record ID number**

4. Change the remaining data types and enter the field descriptions as shown in Figure P2-1, then, designate the **Plant ID field** as the primary key
Next you will enter the data for the table you have just created.

5. Click the **View button** 〔 ▥ ▾ 〕 on the Table Design toolbar, then save the table as **Hydroelectric Plants**
As you begin to enter your data, you decide that you want to include a field that tells the date each plant first became operational. You want it to appear between the River and Kilowatts fields.

6. Switch to the **Design View**, select the **Kilowatts field row**, click the **Insert Rows button** 〔 ᷗᷗ 〕 from the Table Design toolbar, then add the **Operational field** as shown in Figure P2-2
You are now ready to enter your data.

7. Click the **View button** 〔 ▥ ▾ 〕 on the Table Design toolbar to switch to Datasheet View, then enter the data shown in Figure P2-3

8. Save the table

Hint
You can use [Tab] to move to the next cell and [Shift][Tab] to move to the previous cell.

Access 1 Users
Select the Kilowatts field row, click the Insert Row button on the Table Design toolbar, then add the Operational field shown in Figure P2-2.

FIGURE: P2-1: **Hydroelectric Plants table in Design View**

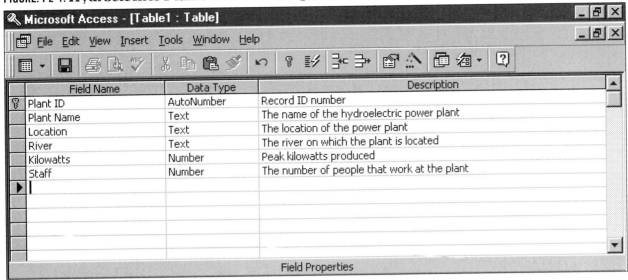

FIGURE P2-2: **Modified for Hydroelectric Plants table**

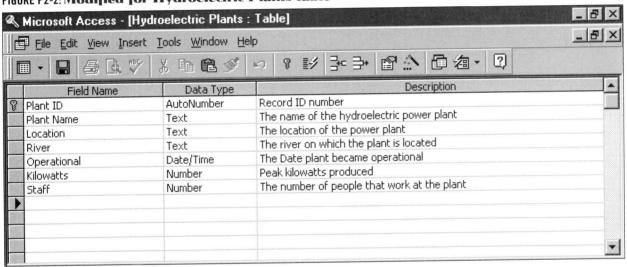

FIGURE: P2-3: **Data records 1 to 11 for the Hydroelectric Plants table**

Plant ID	Plant Name	Location	River	Operational	Kilowatts	Staff
1	Ontario	Canada	Niagara	3/19/35	132500	143
2	Grand Coulee	United States	Columbia	4/24/41	9761000	1045
3	Itaipu	Brazil	Parana	6/4/82	12600000	1430
4	Sir Adam Beck	Canada	Niagara	4/5/29	403900	286
5	Kuybyshev	Russia	Volga	5/8/55	2100000	598
6	Sayano	Russia	Yenisey	6/3/82	6400000	639
7	Beauharnois	Canada	St. Lawrence	4/25/42	1641000	409
8	Volgograd	Russia	Volga	5/11/58	2543000	501
9	Hoover	United States	Colorado	4/19/36	52000	110
10	Bratsk	Russia	Angara	5/17/64	4500000	597
11	Krasnoyarsk	Russia	Yenisey	5/21/68	6096000	710
oNumber)					0	0

HYDROELECTRIC GENERATING PLANTS FOR A LOCAL ORATORS GROUP

activity:

Find and Edit Records, and Create a Custom Query

Upon reviewing the data you have entered into the Hydroelectric Plants table, you have noticed that two of the entries are incorrect. You need to locate and edit this record, and then you will create two custom queries to analyze your data in preparation for writing your speech. You want the first query to calculate the number of years each plant has been in operation. With the second query, you want to calculate the total kilowatts produced and total people employed by these plants.

Hint

If you had multiple plant entries with that name, you could locate the next occurrence by clicking on the Find Next button.

steps:

1. Click any cell in the Plant Name column, click the **Find button** 🔍 on the Table Datasheet toolbar, type **hoover**, remove the check mark from the **Match Case check box** (if necessary), click **Find First**, click **Close**, then change the kilowatt entry for the Hoover record from 52000 to **152000**
You have two other records to update.

2. Change the operational date for the plant named **Ontario** from 3/19/35 to **3/19/30**, change the operational date for the plant named **Sir Adam Beck** from 4/5/29 to **4/5/32**, then save and close the table
Having corrected your data, you are now ready to create your query.

3. Click the **Queries tab**, click **New**, click **Design View**, and from the Show Table dialog box, add the **Hydroelectric Plants** table, then click **Close**
You can now select which fields you would like to display in your query.

4. From the Hydroelectric Plants field list box, select all the fields except **Plant ID** by double-clicking their field names
As part of your query, you would like to calculate the total length of time each plant has been in operation.

5. In the Query Design grid, click the first blank **Field cell**, then type **Years: DateDiff("yyyy", [Operational], Now())**
Before you save and close your query, you would like to sort it in descending order by operational date.

6. Click the **Sort cell** for the **Operational** field, click the **list arrow**, click **Descending**, run the query, then save the query as **Years Analysis**
Your grid should match the one shown in Figure P2-4. Next, you would like to create a query from which you can calculate the total kilowatts produced by, and the total number of persons needed to staff each power plant. This information will help you prepare your speech on Hydroelectric Plants.

7. Create a new query using Design View, add the **Hydroelectric Plants table**, then from the field list box add the fields **Location**, **Kilowatts**, and **Staff** to the Design grid

8. If necessary, click the **Totals button** Σ on the Query Design toolbar to display the Total row on the Query Design grid, click the **Total cell** for the **Kilowatts** field, click **Sum** from the list box, click the **Total cell** for the **Staff field**, then click **Sum** from the list box
Your Design View screen should resemble the one shown in Figure P2-5.

9. Click the **Run button** ❗ on the Query Design toolbar to run the query, save the query as **Location Totals**, then close the query

FIGURE P2-4: Years Analysis query in Design View

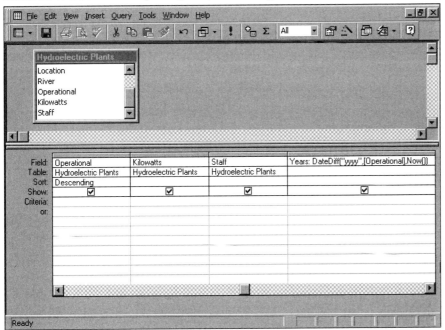

FIGURE P2-5: Location Totals query in Design View

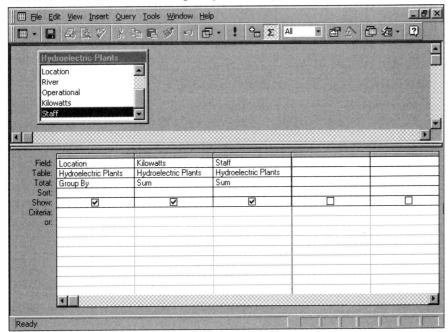

Clues to Use

Working in the Find in field dialog box

You will notice that the title bar of the Find in field dialog box identifies the field you are searching. Type your search text in the Find What text box. Use the Search list box to instruct Access to search All the records in the table, Down the list from the current record, or Up the list from the current record. The Match list box options allow you to match any part of the field ("cap" finds "incapable" and "recap"), the whole field ("long" finds "long" but not "longer"), or the start of a field ("man" finds "manly" but not "woman"). You can also instruct Access to match the case of your search entry ("new" finds "new" but not "New"), search the find data based on its formatting ("1/5/98" finds "1/5/98" but not "05-Jan-98"), or search only the entries in the current field (as opposed to searching all fields in all records) by selecting the appropriate check box.

activity:

Create a Custom Report

Having created the custom queries, you are ready to create a custom report. You've decided you want to distribute the report at your presentation, so you want it to look attractive.

steps:

1. Using **Report Wizard**, create a new report based on the **Years Analysis** query

You now need to select the fields you would like to add to your report.

2. Select all available fields, then click **Next**

Next you will need to specify whether you would like to group and sort the report. You would like the report to group the plants based on which country they are located in and have the detail for each group sorted in ascending order of when they became operational.

3. Group the report on the **Location** field, then sort the report in **ascending order** by the **Operational** field

Having grouped and sorted your report, you can now indicate which fields you would like to have summed on the report. While you have already calculated this information in your custom query, you would like this information to also appear on your report.

4. Click **Summary Options**, click the **Sum check box** for the **Kilowatts** and **Staff** fields, click the **Calculate percent of total for sums check box**, compare your screen with Figure P2-6, then click **OK**

You can now format the basic elements of your report.

5. Click **Next**, select the **Outline 1** layout and **Portrait** orientation, make sure the **Adjust the field width so all fields fit on a page check box** is selected, then click **Next**

With the basic layout of your report specified, you now need to select a report style and title your custom report.

6. Choose the **Corporate** style, title the report **Hydroelectric Plants**, then click **Finish**

Though you have finished creating the report using Report Wizard, you will need to modify its layout using Design View.

7. Switch to **Design View**, and using the Design grid, modify the report layout so that the report resembles the one shown in Figure P2-7

With your report design completed, you can now preview the report and print it.

8. Switch to **Print Preview** by clicking on the **View button** on the Report Design toolbar, then view and print the report

9. Save and close your report, then close the database

FIGURE P2-6: **Summary Options dialog box**

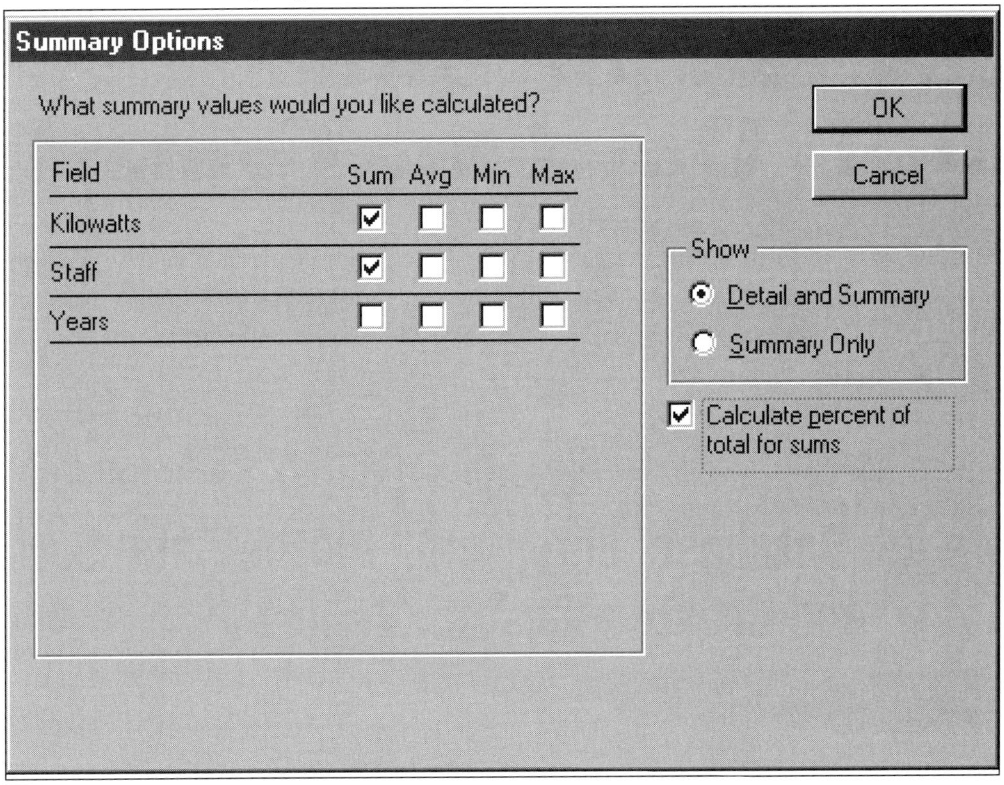

Summary Options

What summary values would you like calculated?

Field	Sum	Avg	Min	Max
Kilowatts	☑	☐	☐	☐
Staff	☑	☐	☐	☐
Years	☐	☐	☐	☐

OK

Cancel

Show
- ● <u>D</u>etail and Summary
- ○ <u>S</u>ummary Only

☑ Calculate <u>p</u>ercent of total for sums

FIGURE P2-7: **Hydroelectric Plants report**

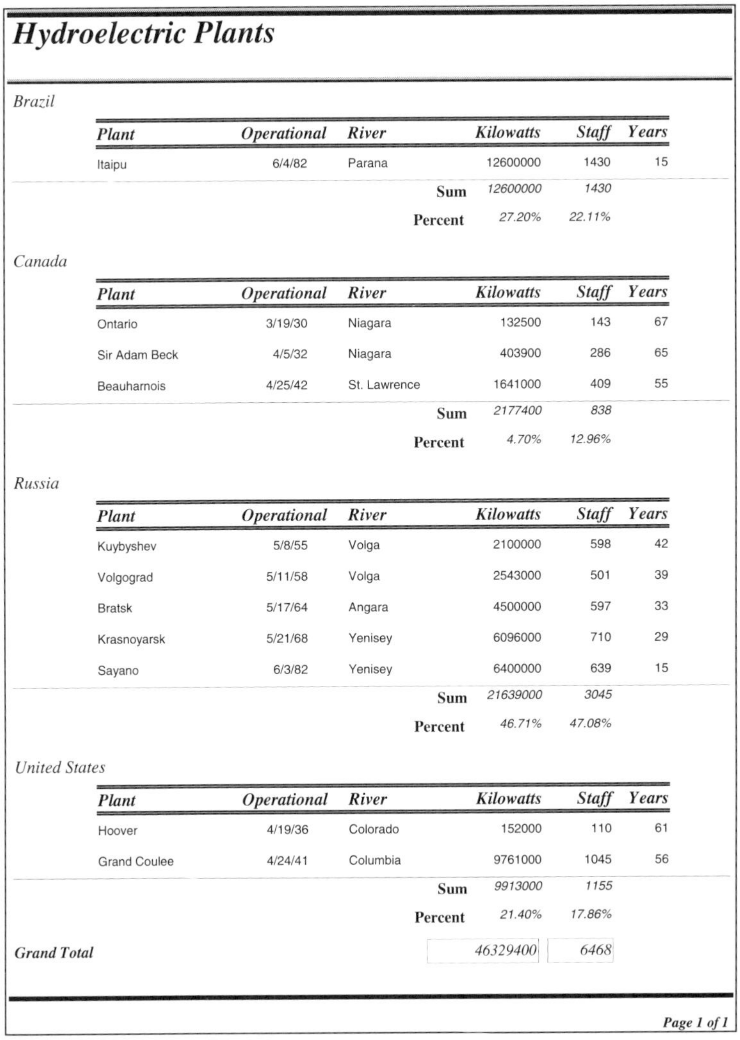

Hydroelectric Plants

Brazil

Plant	Operational	River	Kilowatts	Staff	Years
Itaipu	6/4/82	Parana	12600000	1430	15
		Sum	12600000	1430	
		Percent	27.20%	22.11%	

Canada

Plant	Operational	River	Kilowatts	Staff	Years
Ontario	3/19/30	Niagara	132500	143	67
Sir Adam Beck	4/5/32	Niagara	403900	286	65
Beauharnois	4/25/42	St. Lawrence	1641000	409	55
		Sum	2177400	838	
		Percent	4.70%	12.96%	

Russia

Plant	Operational	River	Kilowatts	Staff	Years
Kuybyshev	5/8/55	Volga	2100000	598	42
Volgograd	5/11/58	Volga	2543000	501	39
Bratsk	5/17/64	Angara	4500000	597	33
Krasnoyarsk	5/21/68	Yenisey	6096000	710	29
Sayano	6/3/82	Yenisey	6400000	639	15
		Sum	21639000	3045	
		Percent	46.71%	47.08%	

United States

Plant	Operational	River	Kilowatts	Staff	Years
Hoover	4/19/36	Colorado	152000	110	61
Grand Coulee	4/24/41	Columbia	9761000	1045	56
		Sum	9913000	1155	
		Percent	21.40%	17.86%	

| *Grand Total* | | | 46329400 | 6468 | |

Book List for Little Angels Day Care Center

Diana Davis, the owner of Little Angels Day Care, would like to create a children's library at her center. As her new assistant, Diana has asked you to catalog the center's list of children's books. To accomplish this task, you will **create a database**, **create a database table**, **enter and edit records**, **sort the records**, and then **create a custom report**.

activities:

Create the Database, Enter and Edit the Data, Sort the Table, and Create a Custom Report

steps:

1. Create a database called **Little Angels Book List** on the disk where you are storing your files for this book

   Having created the database, you can now define a table and designate a primary key. You will use the ISBN Number field as the primary key. While this field is called a number in the field name, there is no consistent format for this number. Because of this, you will define it as a Text field .

2. Using Design View, create the table shown in Figure P3-1, designating the **ISBN Number field** as the primary key, then save the table as **Book List**

   You can now enter your data.

3. Switch to **Datasheet View**, then enter the data shown in Figure P3-2

   After reviewing your entries, you notice some errors that you need to correct.

4. Save the table

Hint

You can change all the necessary records at once using the Replace command on the Edit menu.

5. Change the author's last name from **Pete** to **Peet**

   You can now sort the table.

6. Sort the table in **ascending order** by **Last** name, then save and close it

   Next you can create the custom report.

7. Using **Report Wizard**, create the report shown in Figure P3-3; group the report on the **Last** field; sort the report in **ascending order** by the **Title** field; select the **Stepped** layout and **Portrait** orientation; select the **Corporate** style; and name the report **Little Angels Book List by Author**

8. Print the report, then close the report and the database

FIGURE P3-1: Book List table in Design View

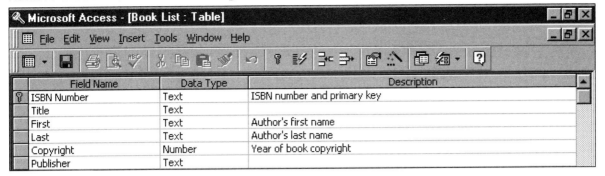

FIGURE P3-2: Data records 1 to 10 for the Book List table

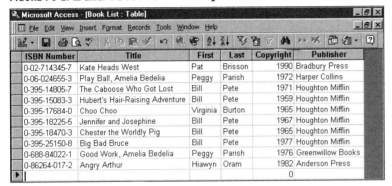

FIGURE P3-3: Little Angels Book List by Author report

Little Angels Book List by Author

Last	Title	ISBN Number	Copyright	Publisher
Brisson				
	Kate Heads West	0-02-714345-7	1990	Bradbury Press
Burton				
	Choo Choo	0-395-17684-0	1965	Houghton Mifflin
Oram				
	Angry Arthur	0-86264-017-2	1982	Anderson Press
Parish				
	Good Work, Amelia Bedeli	0-688-84022-1	1976	Greenwillow Books
	Play Ball, Amelia Bedelia	0-06-024655-3	1972	Harper Collins
Peet				
	Big Bad Bruce	0-395-25150-8	1977	Houghton Mifflin
	Chester the Worldly Pig	0-395-18470-3	1965	Houghton Mifflin
	Hubert's Hair-Raising Adve	0-395-15083-3	1959	Houghton Mifflin
	Jennifer and Josephine	0-395-18225-5	1967	Houghton Mifflin
	The Caboose Who Got Lo	0-395-14805-7	1971	Houghton Mifflin

Independent Challenges

INDEPENDENT CHALLENGE 1

You operate a small business, Deveureux Computers, that sells computer printers and plotters. You want to create a relational database of your products and prepare a list with prices for your customers to review. Since you expect a small drop in the prices of both printers and plotters within the next month, you want to create a query so that you can decide how best to pass these decreases to your customers and remain competitive.

1. In the box below, identify the tables, fields, and table relationships you need for this database.

Tables	Fields	Primary Key	Linking Field

2. Create a relational database called "Deveureux Computers" for tracking information on 15 to 18 products that fall into two categories, printers and plotters, and are each priced at $200 or more. (*Hint: Computer trade magazines are a great resource for locating current model numbers, product names, and prices.*)
3. Create, format, and print a report that lists all products in order by type of product and sorts them by product name.
4. Create a query that calculates a 15% decrease in prices of all products and that also calculates a flat decrease of $100 on each product, then print the query.
5. Save and close the query, then close your database.

INDEPENDENT CHALLENGE 2

You own Northbay Realtors, Inc., which sells residential properties. You want to create a database table that tracks property listings in your locale by city or town. You want this database to include information commonly asked by buyers, such as asking price and the number of bedrooms and bathrooms.

1. In the box below, identify the fields and field properties you need for this database table.

Fields	Data Type	Primary Key

2. Create a database called "Northbay Realtors" and a table named "Property Listings" that contains information on 20 properties for at least 5 to 10 towns or cities in your locale. (*Hint: The classified section of your local newspaper is a good source for obtaining information on properties for sale.*)

3. Create a query named "Available Properties" that includes all the fields from your database table and also includes a calculated field that calculates a 15% down payment on each property and a calculated field that calculates the amount to be financed on each property.

4. Create a query named "Location Averages" that groups properties by location and that calculates the average asking price, number of bedrooms, and number of bathrooms by location.

5. Create, format, and print a report that groups properties by location, lists properties in order by asking price, and calculates the average asking price, average number of bedrooms, average number of bathrooms, average down payment, and average amount to be financed by location.

6. Save and close your report, then close the database.

INDEPENDENT CHALLENGE 3

As the new owner of Compton Computers, a small retail computer outlet, you've restructured the layout of your shelves and products. Your store carries the usual PC-related items: VGA monitors; laser, dot matrix, and ink jet printers; scanners; hard disk, floppy, and CD drives; and an assortment of programs such as Access, Excel, Word, WordPerfect, and Lotus 1-2-3. You have organized your shelves by number and have designated alphabetic sections for each shelf. You have also given each stock item a unique part number. For example, Item 1234 sits in section B of shelf 22; item 5678 sits in section B of shelf 5; and item 9012 sits in section B of shelf 16. You would now like to create a database to help you track and maintain your inventory by its location within the store. From this data, you would like to create a daily report that shows you by part number, the name of each part, its location within the store, and the total quantity on hand of each item. You will use this report to better assist your customers in finding the items they need.

1. Create a database called "Inventory".
2. Use the form provided below to assist you in designing an Item Location table.

> **How are my shelves labeled?** _____
>
> _____
>
> **How are the different sections for each shelf identified?** _____
>
> _____
>
> **What will I use as the primary key?** _____
>
> _____
>
> **What other pieces of data, such as item name, will I need to maintain in my database?** ____
>
> _____

3. Create a table named "Items and Locations" to maintain the data about your inventory.
4. Add at least 15 records to the Items and Locations table. Do not put two items in the same section of the same shelf, and be careful not to put all your items on one shelf.
5. Create a report called "Inventory" that is sorted by item number, calculates the total quantity of each item in the store, and shows where within the store each item is located.
6. After printing the report, save and close your report, then close the database.

INDEPENDENT CHALLENGE 4

As the accounts receivable clerk for Fitzgerald Hospital, a small convalescent facility, you would like to use Access to help you track and report delinquent patient bill payments. To do so, you have decided to create a table to maintain such information as patient information, billing description (the type of treatment they received), billing date, and billing amount. You realize that it is possible for patients to have more than one outstanding bill and have decided to give each receivable its own unique identifier. From this table, you would like to print a report of all patient bills that are 90 days or more past due.

1. Create a database called "Fitzgerald Receivables".
2. Use the form provided below to assist you in planning a table with which to maintain your data.

What field(s) can I use to uniquely identify each receivable? _____

What field(s) can I use to store information about the patient? _____

What field(s) can I use to store information about each bill? _____

What field(s) can I use to determine if a bill is 90 days or more past due? _____

3. Create a table called "Receivables".
4. Develop and enter data for between 10 and 15 patient bill records. Be sure to include some records whose billing date is at least 90 days prior to today's date.
5. Create a query that shows all bills that are 90 days or more past due. To do so, you will need to create a calculated field that calculates the number of days between the billing date and today's date (*Now()*). You can then enter a criteria for this field that will display only those records where the number of days are greater than or equal to 90 days (*>=90*).
6. Create a report named "Past Due" that is sorted by patient name and lists all past due bills and the total amount past due by patient.
7. Save and close your report, then close the database.

Visual Workshop

Use Figure VW-1 to create a table called "Vendors and Subs" in a database called "VGS Contractors", then create the custom report shown in Figure VW-2.

FIGURE VW-1: Vendors and Subs table

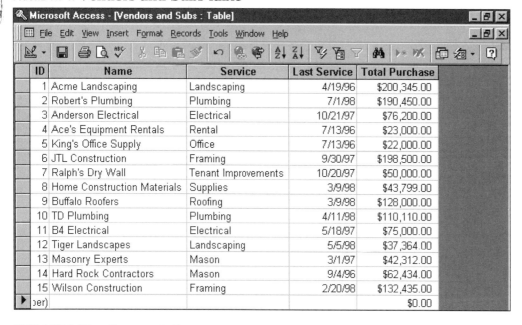

FIGURE VW-2: Vendors and Subs Report

Vendors and Subs Report

Electrical

Name	Last Service	Total Purchase
Anderson Electrical	10/21/97	$76,200.00
B4 Electrical	5/18/97	$75,000.00

Summary for 'Service' = Electrical (2 detail records)

Sum	$151,200.00
Avg	$75,600.00
Percent	10.86%

Framing

Name	Last Service	Total Purchase
JTL Construction	9/30/97	$198,500.00
Wilson Construciton	2/20/98	$132,435.00

Summary for 'Service' = Framing (2 detail records)

Sum	$330,935.00
Avg	$165,467.50
Percent	23.77%

Landscaping

Name	Last Service	Total Purchase
Acme Landscaping	4/19/96	$200,345.00
Tiger Landscapes	5/5/98	$37,364.00

Summary for 'Service' = Landscaping (2 detail records)

Sum	$237,709.00
Avg	$118,854.50
Percent	17.08%

Mason

Name	Last Service	Total Purchase
Hard Rock Contractors	9/4/96	$62,434.00
Masonry Experts	3/1/97	$42,312.00

Summary for 'Service' = Mason (2 detail records)

Sum	$104,746.00
Avg	$52,373.00
Percent	7.53%

Page 1 of 3

Microsoft
► Access
Projects

Professional Databases

In This Unit You Will Create And Work With:

 ► **Protected Species Database**

 ► **Ace Commercial Properties Database**

 ► **Warren Veterinary Hospital Pathology Analyses**

If you work as a self-employed professional or consultant, or for a business, corporation, or federal or state government, you can use Access to track and report on information critical to your profession or business endeavor. For example, if you work as a biologist, you can use databases to keep track of and analyze data that you derive from experiments. If you work as a realtor, you can track property listings for your clients, and keep track of the clients themselves. If you work as a veterinarian or as a pathologist for a hospital, you can use databases to track and report on information from tissue analyses. No matter what field you work in, you will also find Access invaluable for tracking business expenses and depreciation so that you can deduct these expenses from your income taxes. ► In this unit you will learn how to use Microsoft Access to create and work with general business databases. You will create relational and non-relational database tables, create queries with calculated fields that use simple formulas and built-in functions, and create and customize reports to present your information effectively.

Protected Species Database

Clayton Walsh works as a biologist for the state of Texas. One of his new responsibilities is to develop a database that provides information on the status of threatened and endangered animal species whose territories include the state of Texas and the southwestern states. As his research associate, you have checked the Federal Register on the World Wide Web for the latest information on threatened and endangered animals in the Southwestern United States. In order to maintain this information in a form that you can update regularly, you decide to create a database that tracks threatened and endangered mammals.

Project Activities

Create a Relational Database

You will create a Protected Species database with a table for tracking information on endangered or threatened mammals. The second table will contain a list of protected species status codes and their meanings. You will establish a relationship between the two tables based on the species status code.

Update and Sort the Mammals Table

Next, you will update the Mammals table by adding new records and updating the status information on some of the protected mammals. To simplify this process, you will use the search-and-replace features to quickly update the table. Then, you will sort the table by the mammal's common name.

Modify the Database Structure

To expand the usefulness of the Mammals table, you will insert two additional fields and define their properties.

Format and Print a Report

You will use the Report Wizard to produce a formatted report that organizes the mammals by their status (Endangered or Threatened), species name, and then common name.

When you have completed Project 1, your Protected Species report will appear similar to the one shown in Figure P1-1.

FIGURE P1-1: Protected Species report

Protected Species

Species Status Endangered

Species Aplodontia

Common Name	Range	Population
Mountain Beaver, Point ArenaCA		

Species Canis

Common Name	Range	Population
Wolf, Red	Southeast	270

Species Dipodomys

Common Name	Range	Population
Kangaroo Rat, Fresno	CA	
Kangaroo Rat, Giant	CA	
Kangaroo Rat, Morro Bay	CA	
Kangaroo Rat, Stephens	CA	
Kangaroo Rat, Tipton	CA	

Species Felis

Common Name	Range	Population
Jaguarundi	AZ, TX	
Ocelot	AZ, TX	80

Species Leptonycteris

Common Name	Range	Population
Bat, Mexican Long-Nosed	NM, TX	
Bat, Sanborn's Long-Nosed	AZ, NM	

Species Panthera

Common Name	Range	Population
Jaguar	AZ, NM, TX	

Tuesday, April 15, 1997 Page 1 of 2

Species Perognathus

Common Name	Range	Population
Mouse, Pacific Pocket	CA	

Species Reithrodontomys

Common Name	Range	Population
Mouse, Salt Marsh Harvest	CA	

Species Tamiasciurus

Common Name	Range	Population
Squirrel, Mount Graham Red	AZ	

Species Vulpes

Common Name	Range	Population
Fox, San Joaquin Kit	CA	

Species Status Threatened

Species Arctocephalus

Common Name	Range	Population
Seal, Guadalupe Fur	CA	

Species Enhydra

Common Name	Range	Population
Otter, Southern Sea	CA, OR, WA	2100

Species Eumetopias

Common Name	Range	Population
Sea Lion, Stellar	AK, CA, OR, WA	

Species Ursus

Common Name	Range	Population
Bear, Louisiana Brown	LA, MS, TX	300

Tuesday, April 15, 1997 Page 2 of 2

activity:

Create a Relational Database

You start your project by planning the database tables, table fields, primary keys, and linking field. In the first table, you'll include status codes to indicate whether the mammal is "Endangered" or "Threatened." In the second table, you'll include fields for the common name, species name, range, and status, as well as an ID field, for each mammal. After you create these tables, you will link them on a common field.

steps:

1. Start Access, create a database named **Protected Species** on the disk where you are saving your files for this book, click **New** on the Tables sheet, double-click **Design View** in the New Table dialog box, then maximize the Design View window

   Now you can define the fields for the first table.

2. In the first Field Name cell, type **Status**, press **[Enter]** twice to store the fieldname and to select the **Text** Data Type, type **Status code** in the Description cell, click the **Status row selector**, click the **Primary Key button** on the Table Design toolbar, click in the next Field Name cell, type **SpeciesStatus**, press **[Enter]** twice, type **Status of species** in the Description cell, click in the Caption cell on the General Field Properties sheet, then type **Species Status**

   Now you can save the table and enter the two status codes currently used for protected species.

3. Click the **View button** on the Table Design toolbar, and when prompted to save, click **Yes**, type **Species Status** in the Save As dialog box, click **OK**, and after Access switches to Datasheet View, type **E**, press **[Enter]**, type **Endangered**, press **[Enter]**, type **T**, press **[Enter]**, then type **Threatened**

   After you save and close this table, you can create the table that tracks information on protected mammals.

4. Save, then close the Species Status

Hint

Double-click the border between fields to widen fields so that they accommodate the longest entry.

5. Click **New** on the Tables tab in the Database window, double-click **Design View** in the New Table dialog box, maximize the Design View window; enter the field names, select each field's data type, and enter field descriptions using Figure P1-2 as a guideline, set the ID field as the primary key, change the caption of the CommonName field to **Common Name**, then save the table as **Mammals**

   Now you are ready to enter information on 20 threatened and endangered species.

6. Switch to Datasheet view, enter the data on the threatened and endangered species shown in Figure P1-3, then save and close the table

   Now you can define the relationship between the two tables.

Trouble

If Access does not open the Show Table dialog box, click the Show Table button on the Relationships toolbar.

7. Click the **Relationships button** on the Database toolbar, and when the Show Table dialog box opens, double-click **Mammals** in the list box, double-click **Species Status**, click **Close**, and if Access does not automatically define the relationship, drag a field icon for the Status field from the Species Status field list box to the Status field in the Mammals field list box, then release the mouse button, and click **Create** in the Relationships dialog box

8. Save the relationship, then close the Relationships window

FIGURE P1-2: **Mammals table in Design view**

Primary key

New field size for
Status field

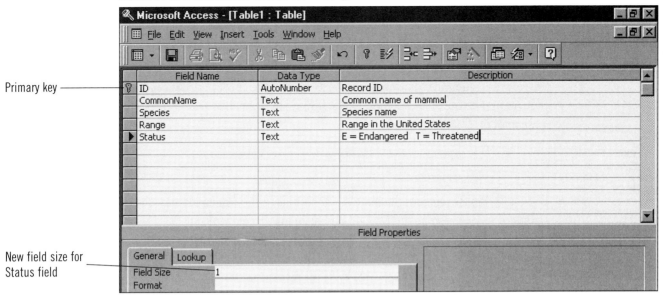

FIGURE P1-3: **Data for records 1 to 18 in the Mammals table**

ID	Common Name	Species	Range	Status
1	Bat, Mexican Long-Nosed	Leptonycteris	NM, TX	E
2	Bear, Louisiana Brown	Ursus	LA, MS, TX	T
3	Fox, San Joaquin Kit	Vulpes	CA	E
4	Jaguar	Panthera	AZ, NM, TX	E
5	Jaguarundi	Felis	AZ, TX	E
6	Kangaroo Rat, Fresno	Dipodimys	CA	E
7	Kangaroo Rat, Giant	Dipodimys	CA	E
8	Kangaroo Rat, Morro Bay	Dipodimys	CA	E
9	Kangaroo Rat, Stephens	Dipodimys	CA	E
10	Kangaroo Rat, Tipton	Dipodimys	CA	E
11	Mountain Beaver, Point Arena	Aplodontia	CA	E
12	Mouse, Pacific Pocket	Perognathus	CA	E
13	Mouse, Salt Marsh Harvest	Reithrodontomys	CA	E
14	Otter, Southern Sea	Enhydra	CA, OR, WA	T
15	Sea Lion, Stellar	Eumetopias	AK, CA, OR, WA	T
16	Seal, Gudalupe Fur	Arctocephalus	CA	T
17	Squirrel, Mount Graham Red	Tamiasciurus	AZ	E
18	Wolf, Red	Canis	Southeast	E

Record: 19 of 19

Common name of mammal

Clues to Use

Using Copy and Paste

If you need to enter the same information repeatedly, such as the same species name, you can copy and paste the information. Simply select the data you want to copy, click the Copy button on the Table Datasheet toolbar, click the record where you want to copy to, then click the Paste button .

activity:

Update and Sort the Mammals Table

After entering the record for the Red Wolf in the Mammals table, you realize you forgot to include two records. You need to add those two records, and then proof the data entry. As you discover errors, you will update the table by finding and editing an individual record or by using Replace to update more than one record at a time.

Hint

In a large database with hundreds or thousands of records, your pointer could be positioned on any record. This technique quickly moves the pointer and inserts a new record.

steps:

1. In the Database window, double-click **Mammals** in the Tables list box, then click the **Blank (New) Record button** ▶* on the Navigation bar to insert a new record

   As you enter the last record, you realize you can save time by copying data from another record.

2. Press **[Enter]**, type **Bat, Sanborn's Long-Nosed**, press **[Enter]**, click the **First Record button** ◄ , double-click the Species name **Leptonycteris** in the first record to highlight it (if necessary), click the **Copy button** 🗎 , on the Table Datasheet toolbar, click in the Species field in the last record, click the **Paste button** 🗎 , press **[Enter]**, type **AZ, NM**, press **[Enter]**, type **E**, then press **[Enter]**

   The other record you missed contained information on the Ocelot.

3. Press **[Enter]**, type **Ocelot**, press **[Enter]**, type **Felis**, press **[Enter]**, type **AZ, TX**, press **[Enter]**, type **E**, then click the **First Record button** ◄ on the Navigation bar

   After quickly proofing your data entry, you realize that you misspelled "Guadalupe."

4. Click the **Common Name field button**, click the **Find button** 🔍 on the Table Datasheet toolbar, type **Gudalupe** in the Find What box, click the **Match list arrow**, click **Any Part of Field** in Match list, click **Find First**, then click **Close**

   Microsoft Access locates and selects the first record that contains "Gudalupe."

5. Click between the "u" and "d" in Gudalupe, then type **a**

   Access inserts the letter "a" and changes "Gudalupe" to "Guadalupe." Next, you want to use Search and Replace to change every occurrence of "Dipodimys" to "Dipodomys."

6. Click the **Species field button**, click **Edit** on the menu bar, click **Replace**, type **Dipodimys** in the Find What box, press **[Tab]**, type **Dipodomys** in the Replace With box, click **Replace All**, and when Access warns you that you cannot undo this Replace operation, click **Yes** in the message dialog box, then click **Close** in the Replace in field: Species dialog box

   Next, you want to sort the table by Species name.

Time To
✓ **Save**

7. Click the **Common Name field button**, then click the **Sort Ascending button** ↓ on the Table Datasheet toolbar

   Figure P1-4 shows the updated and sorted table.

FIGURE P1-4: **Updated table after adding records and correcting typos**

Records sorted by Common Name

Records added to table

Correct spelling of mammal common name

ID	Common Name	Species	Range	Status
1	Bat, Mexican Long-Nosed	Leptonycteris	NM, TX	E
19	Bat, Sanborn's Long-Nosed	Leptonycteris	AZ, NM	E
2	Bear, Louisiana Brown	Ursus	LA, MS, TX	T
3	Fox, San Joaquin Kit	Vulpes	CA	E
4	Jaguar	Panthera	AZ, NM, TX	E
5	Jaguarundi	Felis	AZ, TX	E
6	Kangaroo Rat, Fresno	Dipodomys	CA	E
7	Kangaroo Rat, Giant	Dipodomys	CA	E
8	Kangaroo Rat, Morro Bay	Dipodomys	CA	E
9	Kangaroo Rat, Stephens	Dipodomys	CA	E
10	Kangaroo Rat, Tipton	Dipodomys	CA	E
11	Mountain Beaver, Point Arena	Aplodontia	CA	E
12	Mouse, Pacific Pocket	Perognathus	CA	E
13	Mouse, Salt Marsh Harvest	Reithrodontomys	CA	E
20	Ocelot	Felis	AZ, TX	E
14	Otter, Southern Sea	Enhydra	CA, OR, WA	T
15	Sea Lion, Stellar	Eumetopias	AK, CA, OR, WA	T
16	Seal, Guadalupe Fur	Arctocephalus	CA	T
17	Squirrel, Mount Graham Red	Tamiasciurus	AZ	E
18	Wolf, Red	Canis	Southeast	E

Record: 1 of 20

Correct spelling of Species name

Clues to Use

Indexed fields

Indexed fields simplify and speed up query, sorting, and grouping operations in Access. When you specify an AutoNumber field as the primary key, Access automatically indexes it. AutoNumber fields also facilitate indexing because they do not produce duplicate values. If you want to return a table to its original order, simply sort the AutoNumber field in ascending order.

activity:

Modify the Database Structure

After showing Clayton a copy of the new protected species table, the two of you decide that it would be useful to also include a field that contains an estimate of the population of these mammals, where available, and a field for displaying scanned images of the mammals.

Access 7 Users

Click the Insert Row button after you select the Range row selector

steps:

1. Click the **View button** to switch to Design View

You decide to insert the new field between the Species and Range fields.

2. Click the **Range row selector**, click the **Insert Rows button** on the Table Design toolbar

Access inserts a blank field into the database structure. Now you can define the Population field.

3. Click in the Field Name cell, type **Population** for the new field name, then press **[Enter]**, click the **Data Type list arrow**, then click **Number**, click in the Description cell, type **Number of known individuals in range**, click in the **Field Size cell** of the General Field Properties Sheet, click the **Field Size list arrow**, then click **Integer**

You decide to add the field that will contain a photograph of the mammal after the Status field.

4. Click the **Field Name cell** following the Status field cell, type **Photograph**, press **[Enter]**, click the **Data Type list arrow**, click **OLE Object**, press **[Enter]**, then type **Scanned image**

Your modified database structure should be similar to that shown in Figure P1-5.

5. Click the **View button**, click **Yes** to save changes to the database

Next, you can enter information on population sizes for those species for which you have this information.

6. Click the **Population field** for the Louisiana Brown Bear and type **300**; click the **Population field** for the Ocelot and type **80**; click the **Population field** for the Southern Sea Otter and type **2100**; click the **Population field** for the Red Wolf and type **270**

Figure P1-6 shows the updated table. Later, you can add scanned photos of each mammal.

7. Save and close the table

FIGURE P1-5: Modified database structure of the Mammals table

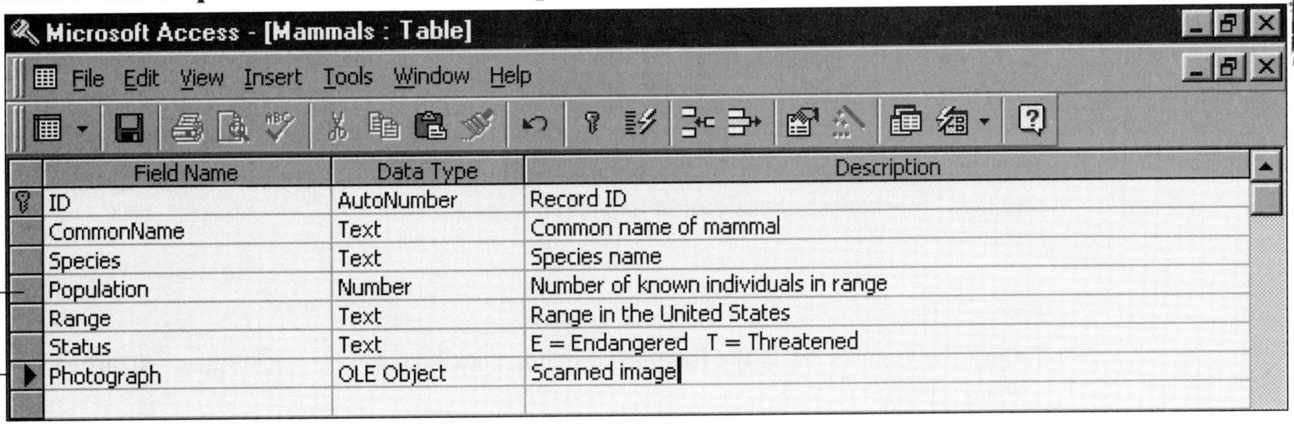

Microsoft Access - [Mammals : Table]

File   Edit   View   Insert   Tools   Window   Help

	Field Name	Data Type	Description
🔑	ID	AutoNumber	Record ID
	CommonName	Text	Common name of mammal
	Species	Text	Species name
	Population	Number	Number of known individuals in range
	Range	Text	Range in the United States
	Status	Text	E = Endangered T = Threatened
▶	Photograph	OLE Object	Scanned image

└─New fields

FIGURE P1-6: Updated Mammals table

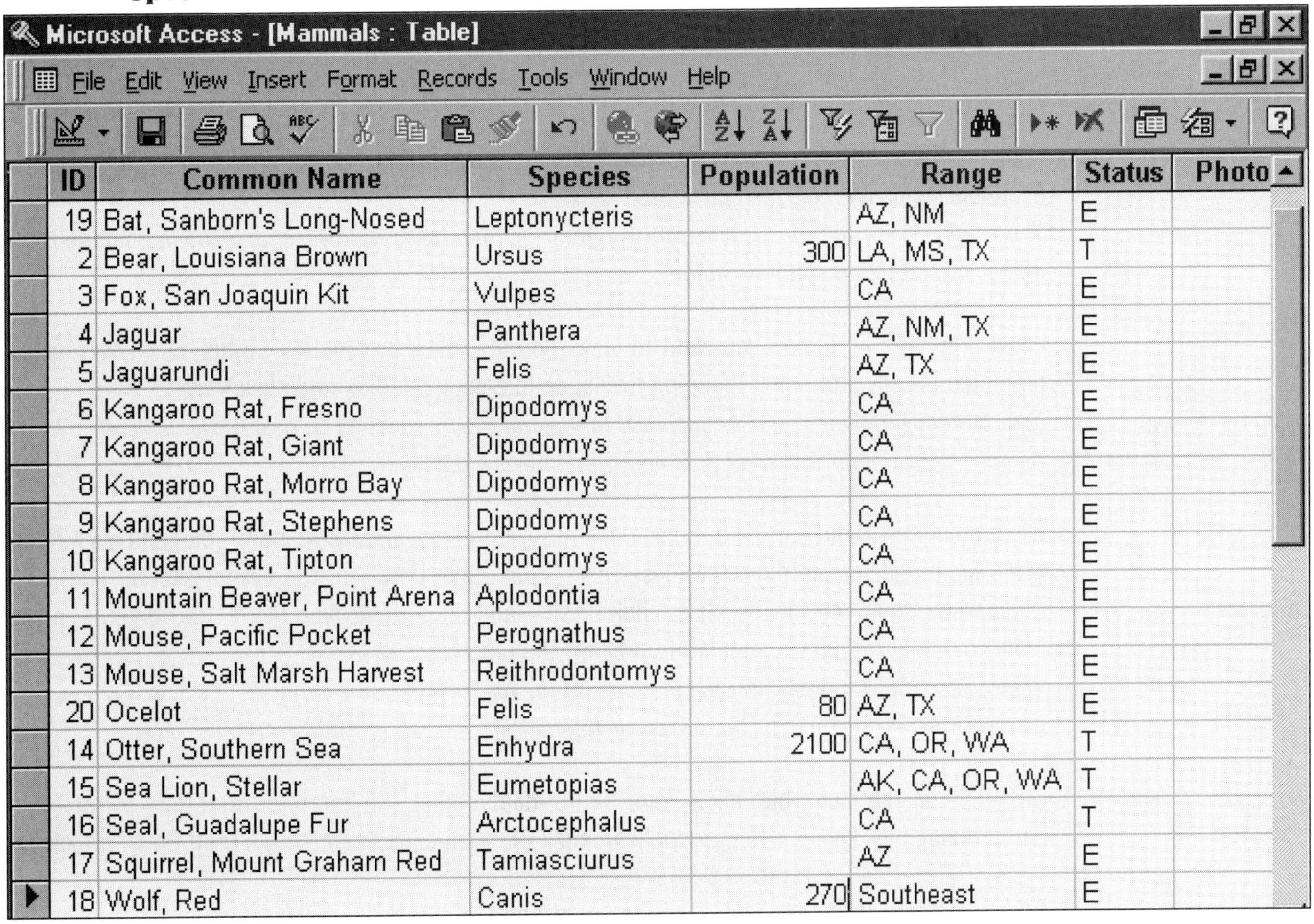

Microsoft Access - [Mammals : Table]

File   Edit   View   Insert   Format   Records   Tools   Window   Help

ID	Common Name	Species	Population	Range	Status	Photo
19	Bat, Sanborn's Long-Nosed	Leptonycteris		AZ, NM	E	
2	Bear, Louisiana Brown	Ursus	300	LA, MS, TX	T	
3	Fox, San Joaquin Kit	Vulpes		CA	E	
4	Jaguar	Panthera		AZ, NM, TX	E	
5	Jaguarundi	Felis		AZ, TX	E	
6	Kangaroo Rat, Fresno	Dipodomys		CA	E	
7	Kangaroo Rat, Giant	Dipodomys		CA	E	
8	Kangaroo Rat, Morro Bay	Dipodomys		CA	E	
9	Kangaroo Rat, Stephens	Dipodomys		CA	E	
10	Kangaroo Rat, Tipton	Dipodomys		CA	E	
11	Mountain Beaver, Point Arena	Aplodontia		CA	E	
12	Mouse, Pacific Pocket	Perognathus		CA	E	
13	Mouse, Salt Marsh Harvest	Reithrodontomys		CA	E	
20	Ocelot	Felis	80	AZ, TX	E	
14	Otter, Southern Sea	Enhydra	2100	CA, OR, WA	T	
15	Sea Lion, Stellar	Eumetopias		AK, CA, OR, WA	T	
16	Seal, Guadalupe Fur	Arctocephalus		CA	T	
17	Squirrel, Mount Graham Red	Tamiasciurus		AZ	E	
18	Wolf, Red	Canis	270	Southeast	E	

activity:

Format and Print a Custom Report

You will use the Report Wizard to create a custom report that lists protected mammals under one of two categories: Endangered, or Threatened. Within each category, you will list mammals by species, and then alphabetically by common name.

steps:

1. Click the **Reports tab** in the Database window, click **New**, double-click **Report Wizard** in the New Report dialog box

   The Report Wizard prompts for the fields to include in the report. You want to include fields from both tables, starting with the Mammals table.

2. Click the **Tables/Queries list arrow** and click **Table: Mammals** (if necessary), double-click **CommonName** in the Available Fields list box, double-click **Species**, double-click **Range**, then double-click **Population**

   Now you can select the fields from the Species Status table.

3. Click the **Tables/Queries list arrow**, click **Table: Species Status**, double-click **SpeciesStatus** in the Available Fields list box, then click **Next**

   You want to view data by Species Status, group the mammals by species, and list the mammals in alphabetical order by common name.

4. When prompted as to how you want to view the data, click **by Species Status**, click **Next**; when prompted for any additional grouping levels, double-click **Species** and click **Next**

   Your grouping options should be identical to those in Figure P1-7. Next, specify the sort order, choose the report layout and style, and then name and preview the report.

5. When prompted about sorting options, click the **1 list arrow**, click **CommonName**, and click **Next**; when prompted for the page layout settings, click **Align Left 1** in the Layout section and click **Next**; when prompted for the style, click **Casual** and click **Next**, type **Protected Species** in the report name box, then click **Finish** to preview the report

   Figure P1-8 shows a preview of the first page of the report. After examining the previewed report, you discover you need to increase the size of the top margin.

6. Click **File** on the menu bar, click **Page Setup**, double-click the **Top margin setting** in the Page Setup dialog box, type **1.5** (for 1½ inches), click **OK**, then click **Close** on the Print Preview toolbar

7. Print the report, then save and close the report and the database

Clues to Use

Default page layout settings

The default page layout settings in Access are a Stepped layout for a grouped report, a Tabular layout for an ungrouped report, Portrait orientation, and the Adjust the field width so all fields fit on one page option.

FIGURE P1-7: Grouping options for the Protected Species report

View data by
SpeciesStatus

Group data
by Species

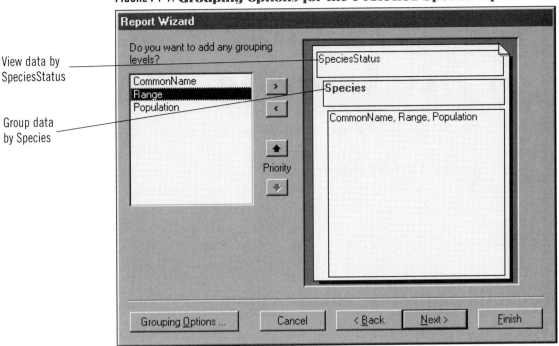

FIGURE P1-8: Preview of the first page of the Protected Species report

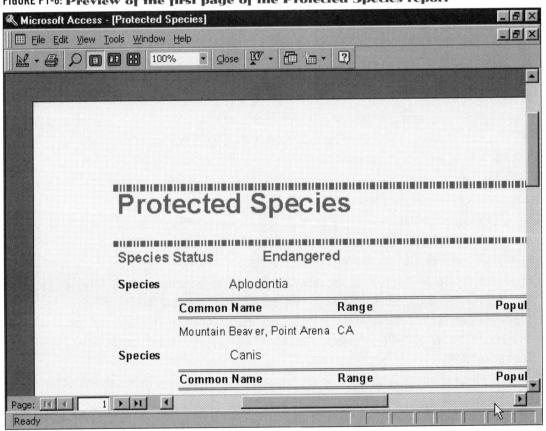

Access 97

Sales Tracking System for Ace Commercial Sales

George "Ace" Peterson owns a real estate business named Ace Commercial Sales which specializes in commercial properties. George has decided to develop a sales reporting system. He will use this system to generate queries and reports that show how individual employees are performing and how property sales are progressing. To create his tracking system, he will **create three database tables**, **establish table relationships**, **query the tables**, and then **modify the query and create a custom report**.

activities:

Create Three Database Tables

To maintain the sales tracking system efficiently, George needs three tables: the first will maintain data regarding sold properties; the second will contain information about the properties sold; and the third will store information about the real estate sales agent who sold the property.

steps:

1. Create a new database based on the **Blank Database template**, name the database **Ace Sales History**, then save it to the disk where you are saving your files
   First, George designs the table that will contain information on sold properties.

2. Use **Table Wizard** to create a new table, click **Order Details** in the Sample Tables list box, double-click **OrderDetailID** and rename it **Sales ID**, double-click **ProductID** and rename it **Agent ID**, double-click **ProductID** again and rename it **Property ID**, double-click **DateSold** and rename it **Sale Date**, double-click **UnitPrice** and rename it **List Price**, double-click **SalePrice** and rename it **Sale Price**, click **Next**, let Access set the primary key, name the table **Sales Detail**, then click **Finish**
   Having defined the Sales Detail table, George can enter the recent real estate sales data.

3. Enter the data shown in Figure P2-1 in the Sales Detail table, then save and close the table
   You now need to create the next table.

4. Using Table Wizard's **Products** sample table, double-click **ProductID**, rename it **Property ID**, double-click **ProductDescription**, then rename it **Description**
   Now you'll use fields from another sample table to complete the table design.

5. From the **Contacts** sample table, double-click **Address**, double-click **City**, double-click **StateOrProvince** and rename it **State**, double-click **PostalCode** and rename it **Zip**, let Access set the primary key for you, name the table **Property Master**, click **Relationships**, set the relationship so that one record in the Property Master table will match many records in the Sales Detail table, then click **Finish**

6. Enter the data shown in Figure P2-2 in the Property Master table, then save and close the table
   You can now create your last table.

7. Using Design View, create a new table named **Agent Master** that contains an AutoNumber field named **Agent ID** (make this field the primary key), a text field named **First Name**, and a text field named **Last Name**

8. Enter the data shown in Figure P2-3 into the Agent Master table, then save and close the table

FIGURE P2-1: Data for records 1 to 12 for the Sales Detail table

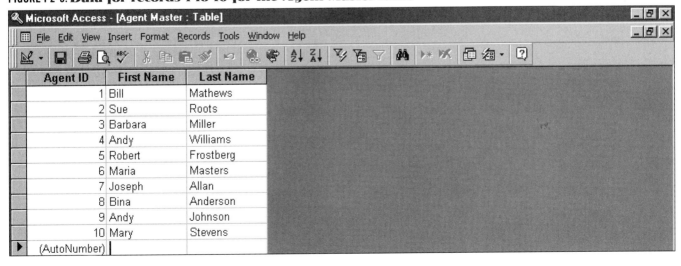

Microsoft Access - [Sales Detail : Table]

File Edit View Insert Format Records Tools Window Help

Sales ID	Agent ID	Property ID	Sale Date	List Price	Sale Price
1	5	1	10/1/97	$185,000.00	$179,500.00
2	4	4	9/14/97	$1,200,000.00	$990,000.00
3	5	10	8/18/98	$347,990.00	$339,900.00
4	2	2	6/6/96	$773,500.00	$773,500.00
5	1	7	11/30/98	$225,000.00	$220,000.00
6	3	3	1/1/98	$89,000.00	$87,500.00
7	7	4	9/14/97	$198,000.00	$195,000.00
8	8	6	2/5/98	$399,999.00	$375,000.00
9	5	1	10/1/97	$380,000.00	$380,000.00
10	4	5	9/25/98	$475,000.00	$395,000.00
11	3	9	4/1/98	$1,400,000.00	$1,375,000.00
12	4	8	2/15/97	$349,900.00	$349,000.00

FIGURE P2-2: Data for records 1 to 10 for the Property Master table

Microsoft Access - [Property Master : Table]

File Edit View Insert Format Records Tools Window Help

Property ID	Description	Address	City	State	Zip
1	35000sf/mfg	123 Main Street	Holmer	CA	92345-
2	2500sf/rest	443 South Street	Westhaven	CA	92434-
3	1800sf/office	10 Downing Ave	Homer	CA	92345-
4	12000sf/office	843 Access Way	Homer	CA	92346-
5	14500sf/lt mfg	3232 Lucy Court	Ruhl	CA	92724-
6	5250sf/retail	933 Millhouse Blvd	Lemon	CA	92666-
7	10000sf/med	55 Ralph Way	Homer	CA	92346-
8	21500sf/ware	8 Compton Street	Ruhl	CA	92724-
9	2500sf/office	112 Lucy Court	Homer	CA	92345-
10	17500sf/mfg	333 Joseph Ave	Westhaven	CA	92434-
(AutoNumber)					

Access provides room for extended zip codes in this field

FIGURE P2-3: Data for records 1 to 10 for the Agent Master table

Microsoft Access - [Agent Master : Table]

File Edit View Insert Format Records Tools Window Help

Agent ID	First Name	Last Name
1	Bill	Mathews
2	Sue	Roots
3	Barbara	Miller
4	Andy	Williams
5	Robert	Frostberg
6	Maria	Masters
7	Joseph	Allan
8	Bina	Anderson
9	Andy	Johnson
10	Mary	Stevens
(AutoNumber)		

activities:

Establish Table Relationships and Create a Custom Query

George wants to create a report showing all sales made by sales agent, sorted in ascending order. He would like the report to include the agent's first and last name, the property number and description, the date the property sold, and the list and sales prices. Before he can create this report however, he needs to establish relationships between the Sales Detail, Property Master, and Agent Master tables, and then create a custom query.

steps:

1. Click the **Relationships button** on the Table Database toolbar, maximize the Relationships window (if necessary), then click the **Show Table button** on the Relationship toolbar (if not currently displayed)

George needs to create relationships among all the tables in the database.

2. In the Show Table dialog box, add the **Agent Master, Sales Detail**, and **Property Master** tables, then click **Close**

You are now ready to establish the relational links.

3. If necessary, drag the **Agent ID field** from the Agent Master field list box to the **Agent ID field** in the Sales Detail field list box, click **Create**; drag the **Property ID field** from the Sales Detail field list box to the **Property ID field** in the Property Master field list box, click **Create**, then click **Close**

Your screen should match the one shown in Figure P2-4.

4. Close the Relationships window, saving your relationships when prompted

Now that you have established the relational links between the tables, you can create the query.

5. Use **Simple Query Wizard** to create a new query

You'll use fields from all the tables in this query.

6. From the Agent Master table, add the **FirstName** and **LastName** fields; from the Property Master table, add the **Property ID** and **Description** fields; from the Sales Detail table add the **Sales Date, List Price**, and **Sales Price** fields, then click **Next**; click **Next** again, name the query **Sales Activity Query**, click the **Modify the query design option button**, then click **Finish**

Before running the query, George wants to sort the selected query by Last Name, so that individual information in the final report is easy to find.

7. Modify the query form to sort in ascending order by **Last Name**

Your select query should match the one shown in Figure P2-5.

8. Save your modified query, and then run it

Compare your query table with Figure P2-6.

FIGURE P2-4: **Table relationships**

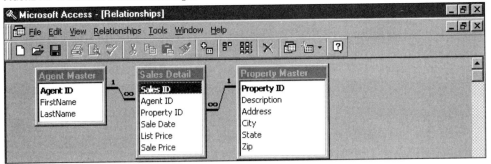

FIGURE P2-5: **Sales Activity Query in Design View**

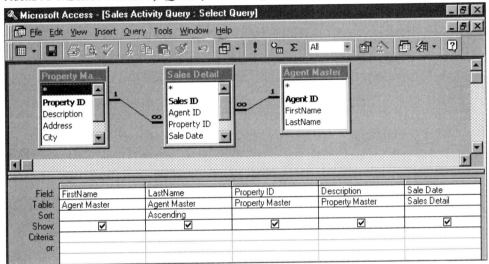

FIGURE P2-6: **Sales Activity Query results in Datasheet View**

First Name	Last Name	Property ID	Description	Sale Date	List Price	Sale Price
Joseph	Allan	4	12000sf/office	9/14/97	$198,000.00	$195,000.00
Bina	Anderson	6	5250sf/retail	2/5/98	$399,999.00	$375,000.00
Robert	Frostberg	1	35000sf/mfg	10/1/97	$380,000.00	$380,000.00
Robert	Frostberg	10	17500sf/mfg	8/18/98	$347,990.00	$339,900.00
Robert	Frostberg	1	35000sf/mfg	10/1/97	$185,000.00	$179,500.00
Bill	Mathews	7	10000sf/med	11/30/98	$225,000.00	$220,000.00
Barbara	Miller	9	2500sf/office	4/1/98	$1,400,000.00	$1,375,000.00
Barbara	Miller	3	1800sf/office	1/1/98	$89,000.00	$87,500.00
Sue	Roots	2	2500sf/rest	6/6/96	$773,500.00	$773,500.00
Andy	Williams	8	21500sf/ware	2/15/97	$349,900.00	$349,000.00
Andy	Williams	5	14500sf/lt mfg	9/25/98	$475,000.00	$395,000.00
Andy	Williams	4	12000sf/office	9/14/97	$1,200,000.00	$990,000.00
		(AutoNumber)				

Clues to Use

Editing table relationships

Access displays a join line between the related table fields. To edit an existing relationship, double-click the center of the join line and, using the drop-down field lists, select which fields are related. From this dialog box, you can also elect whether Access will automatically update or delete corresponding values in the related table whenever you change or delete a primary key value in the primary table. For example, if you change a CustomerID field in the Customer Master table, the CustomerID field in all the Order table records are automatically updated so that the relationship that exists between the two tables isn't broken.

activity:

Modifying a Query and Creating a Custom Report

George needs to create a custom report that displays all sales over $250,000 made by Robert Frostberg in descending order of sales price. To do this, he needs to use Query Design View to modify the existing query, and then use it to create a custom report.

steps:

1. Click the **View button** [icon] on the Query Datasheet toolbar

Using the Design grid, you can define the necessary criteria and sorting instructions needed to complete the report. By entering the criterion "Robert" in the FirstName field, you have requested that Access select only those records whose FirstName field matches that entry.

2. In the Design grid, click the **First Name Criteria cell**, then type **Robert**

Access will automatically add quotation marks around Robert after you complete the entry by pressing [Enter] or [Tab], or by clicking elsewhere in the form.

3. Add the criterion **Frostberg** to the **LastName** field, remove the Ascending sort option from the **LastName** field, add the criterion **>=250000** to the **Sale Price** field, then sort the query in descending order by **Sale Price**

4. Run the query, then save and close it

Your selected query table should match the one shown in Figure P2-7. From here you can create your custom report.

5. Click the **New Object list arrow** [icon] on the Query Database toolbar, click **Report**, click **Report Wizard**, make sure the **Sales Activity Query** is selected in the Tables/Queries list box, add all fields to the report, then click **Next**

6. View the report by **Agent Master**, do not add any grouping levels, do not sort the report, click **Summary Options**, sum the **List Price** and **Sale Price** fields, click **Next**, use the **Align Left 2** layout and a **Landscape** orientation, then click **Next**

7. Select the **Corporate** style, name the report **Robert Frostberg's $250,000+ Sales**, then preview the report

8. Switch to **Design View** and modify your report so it resembles the one shown in Figure P2-8

When you have finished modifying your report, it should closely match the one shown in Figure P2-8.

Time To

✓ **Save**

✓ **Close**

FIGURE P2-7: **Modified Sales Activity Query in Datasheet View**

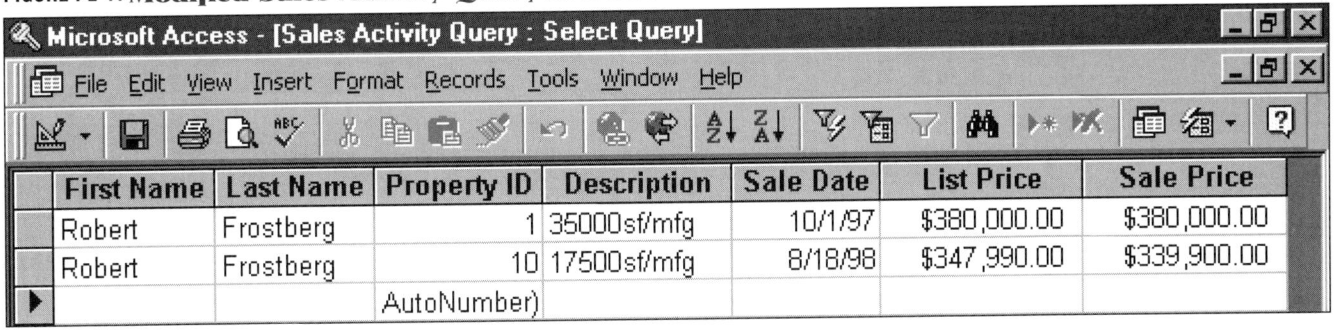

Microsoft Access - [Sales Activity Query : Select Query]

File Edit View Insert Format Records Tools Window Help

First Name	Last Name	Property ID	Description	Sale Date	List Price	Sale Price
Robert	Frostberg	1	35000sf/mfg	10/1/97	$380,000.00	$380,000.00
Robert	Frostberg	10	17500sf/mfg	8/18/98	$347,990.00	$339,900.00
		(AutoNumber)				

FIGURE P2-8: **Robert Frostberg's $250,000+ Sales Report**

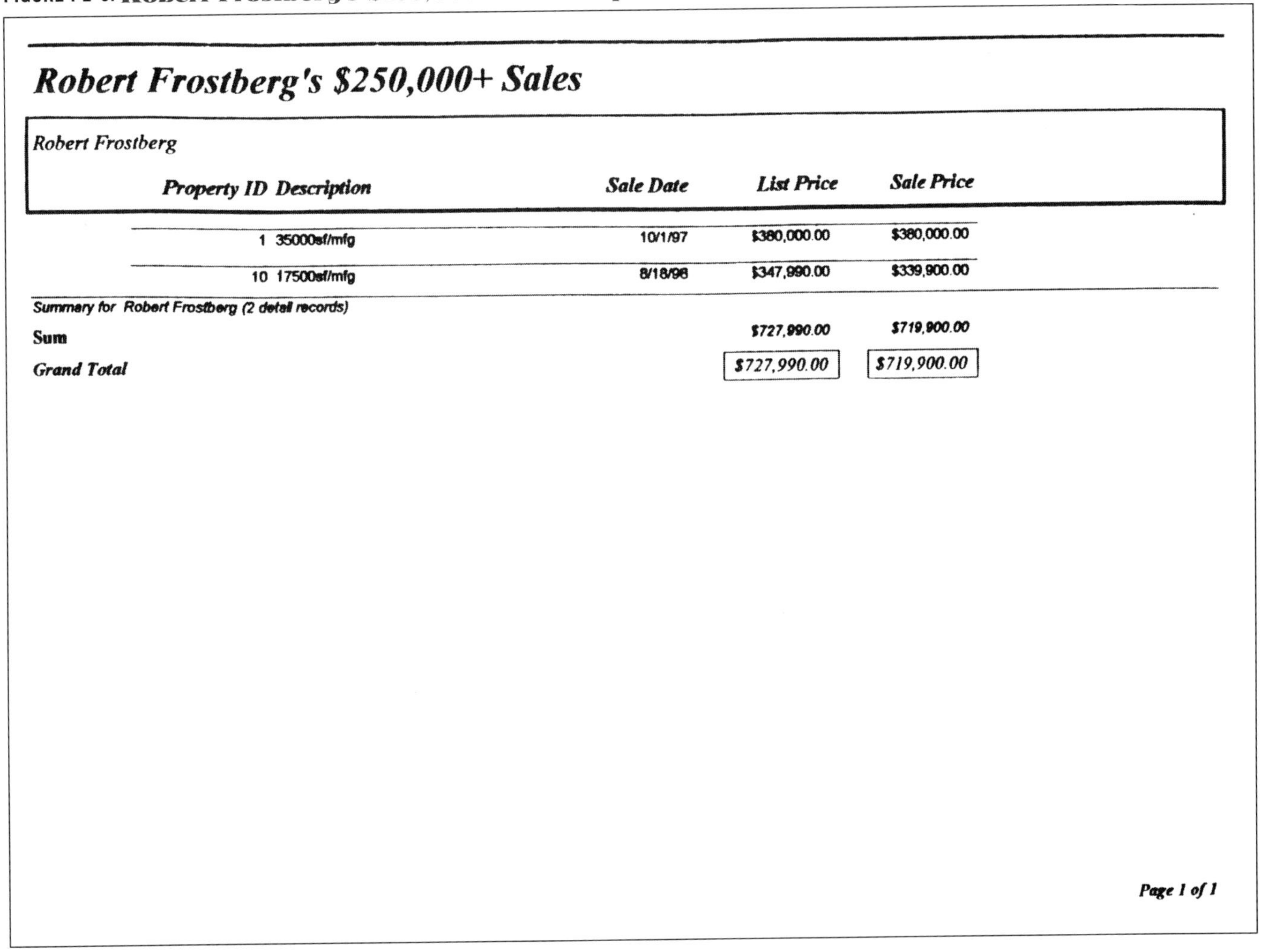

Robert Frostberg's $250,000+ Sales

Robert Frostberg

Property ID	Description	Sale Date	List Price	Sale Price
1	35000sf/mfg	10/1/97	$380,000.00	$380,000.00
10	17500sf/mfg	8/18/98	$347,990.00	$339,900.00

Summary for Robert Frostberg (2 detail records)

Sum $727,990.00 $719,900.00

Grand Total $727,990.00 $719,900.00

Page 1 of 1

Pathology Analysis for Warren Veterinary Hospital

As a state veterinarian, one of your responsibilities is the tracking and reporting of livestock pathogens. You are required by the state to issue a detailed, monthly report, grouped by pathogen class, of all livestock disease occurrences taking place in your geographical area. To help you track and report this necessary information, you will **create a pathogens database, a diseases table**, and an **occurrences table; query these tables**, then **create and print a custom report using these query results**.

activities:

Create Three Related Database Tables, Query the Tables, and Create a Report

steps:

1. Create a database called **Pathogens**, create a table that contains an **ID field** with an **Autonumber Data Type**, (make this the primary key), a **Name field** with a **Text Data Type**, and a **Class field** with a **Text Data Type**, save the table as **Diseases**, enter the data as shown in Figure P3-1, then save and close the table

2. Create a table named **Occurrences** using Figure P3-2, enter the data as shown in Figure P3-3, then close the table

   Having created both tables, you can now establish the necessary relationship.

3. Create a one-to-many relationship between **ID field** in the **Diseases table** and the **Disease ID field** in the Occurrences table

   You can now create the query.

4. Using **Simple Query Wizard**, create a query that shows all fields from the **Diseases table** except **ID**, and the **Location, Qty, Date**, and **Species fields** from the **Occurrences table**

   From this basic query, you can specify criteria that will select only those records for the month of September, 1998.

5. Name the query **Monthly**, and then modify it to display only those occurrences that took place in 9/98 by entering **Between 9/1/98 and 9/30/98** to the **Criteria cell** for the **Date field** in the Design grid

   Access formats the criteria entry as "Between #9/1/98# And #9/30/98#" after you complete the entry. After running the modified query, you'll be ready to create the monthly pathology report.

6. Run the query, then use **Report Wizard** to create a new report that includes the **Name, Class, Date, Location, Qty**, and **Species fields** from the **Monthly** query, view the data by **Diseases**, group the report by **Class**, sort the detail records in ascending date order, sum the **Qty field**, accept the default layout and orientation, select the **Corporate** style, then name the report **Monthly Pathology Report**

7. Using Design View, modify your report to match the one shown in Figure P3-4, print it, then save and close the report and the database

FIGURE P3-1: Records 1 to 5 for Diseases Table

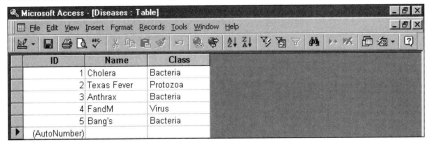

ID	Name	Class
1	Cholera	Bacteria
2	Texas Fever	Protozoa
3	Anthrax	Bacteria
4	FandM	Virus
5	Bang's	Bacteria
(AutoNumber)		

FIGURE P3-2: Design View of Occurrences table

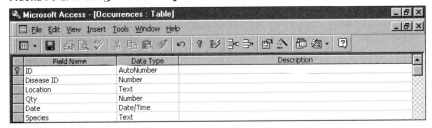

Field Name	Data Type	Description
ID	AutoNumber	
Disease ID	Number	
Location	Text	
Qty	Number	
Date	Date/Time	
Species	Text	

FIGURE P3-3: Records 1 to 15 for the Occurrences table

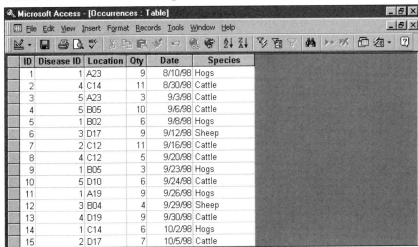

ID	Disease ID	Location	Qty	Date	Species
1	1	A23	9	8/10/98	Hogs
2	4	C14	11	8/30/98	Cattle
3	5	A23	3	9/3/98	Cattle
4	5	B05	10	9/6/98	Cattle
5	1	B02	6	9/8/98	Hogs
6	3	D17	9	9/12/98	Sheep
7	2	C12	11	9/16/98	Cattle
8	4	C12	5	9/20/98	Cattle
9	1	B05	3	9/23/98	Hogs
10	5	D10	6	9/24/98	Cattle
11	1	A19	9	9/26/98	Hogs
12	3	B04	4	9/29/98	Sheep
13	4	D19	9	9/30/98	Cattle
14	1	C14	6	10/2/98	Hogs
15	2	D17	7	10/5/98	Cattle

FIGURE P3-4: Monthly Pathology Report

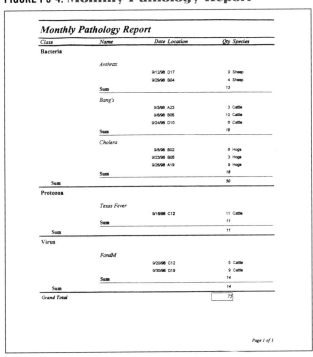

Monthly Pathology Report

Class	Name	Date	Location	Qty	Species
Bacteria					
	Anthrax	9/12/98	D17	9	Sheep
		9/29/98	B04	4	Sheep
	Sum			13	
	Bang's	9/3/98	A23	3	Cattle
		9/6/98	B05	10	Cattle
		9/24/98	D10	6	Cattle
	Sum			19	
	Cholera	9/8/98	B02	6	Hogs
		9/23/98	B05	3	Hogs
		9/26/98	A19	9	Hogs
	Sum			18	
Sum				50	
Protozoa					
	Texas Fever	9/16/98	C12	11	Cattle
	Sum			11	
Sum				11	
Virus					
	FandM	9/20/98	C12	5	Cattle
		9/30/98	D19	9	Cattle
	Sum			14	
Sum				14	
Grand Total				75	

Page 1 of 1

Independent Challenges

As a financial investment counselor, you must file quarterly estimated tax statements for both your federal and state taxes. Since your income fluctuates substantially from quarter to quarter, you file annualized income tax statements so that you do not underpay or overpay taxes for any quarter. To simplify your tax preparation, you want to create a relational database that tracks expenses for advertising, office expenses, online costs, supplies, subscriptions, and utilities for the last two quarters.

1. Using the following form, identify the tables, fields, and table relationships you need for this database:

Tables	Fields	Primary Key	Linking Field

2. Create a relational database called "Schedule C Expenses" that contains 15 different types of expenses incurred during the first two quarters of the year.
3. Update the table by adding 5 to 10 new expenses, and sort the table by expense date.
4. Create, format, and print a report that lists Schedule C expenses first by expense category, and then by quarter. Sort the expenses by expense date.

As the owner of a small business, you depreciate tangible property on your federal and state income taxes. To simplify this process, you decide to create a relational database that tracks expenses for office furniture and fixtures, which have a seven-year useful life, computer hardware and office machinery, which have a five-year useful life, and computer software, which has a three-year useful life. To calculate the depreciation, you must track the date of the purchase. You also want to include the quarter the item was purchased, so that your expense report groups deductible expenses for each quarter that you must file an estimated tax statement.

1. Using the following form, identify the tables, fields, and table relationships you need for this database.

Tables	Fields	Primary Key	Linking Field

2. Create a relational database called "Depreciation" that contains 15 different types of expenses incurred for depreciable properties which have a three-year, five-year, and seven-year useful life.
3. Create a query that includes information on all depreciable expenses, and then modify the query and add a calculated field that determines the amount of the yearly allowable depreciation by dividing the cost of each expense by its useful life (called straight-line depreciation).
4. Create, format, and print a report that lists depreciable expenses first by type of depreciation, and then by quarter. Sort the depreciable expenses by expense date.

INDEPENDENT CHALLENGE 3

You've always wanted to own your own business. This desire, combined with your love of plants and landscaping, has led you to purchase a small, but well-established, nursery specializing in plants, shrubs, and trees that are native to the surrounding area. As the new owner of Elizabeth Young's Native Nursery, you would like to track commercial orders by salesperson. To do so, you have decided to create a database with three tables: The first table, named Order Detail, will maintain data regarding sales orders; the second table, named Item Master, will contain information relative to the items you sell in your Nursery; and the final table, named Salesperson Master, will be used to store and maintain information regarding the sales agent that sold the order.

1. Create a database called "Nursery Sales."
2. Use the form provided below to help you design the Order Detail table (note that the nursery's commercial orders contain one item per order):

> **How will I uniquely identify each sales order record?**
>
> **What kinds of information will I need to track on a sales order?**
>
> **What kinds of information will I need to help track the total sales made by each salesperson?**
>
> **What data type should I assign to each field?**

3. Add 10 records to the Order Detail table.
4. Use the form provided below to help you create the Item Master table:

> **How will I uniquely identify each item?**
>
> **What kinds of information will I need to maintain for each item?**
>
> **Will I need a description for each item?**
>
> **What data type should I assign to each field?**

5. Add 10 items to the Item Master table.
6. Use the form provided below to help you create the Salesperson Master table:

> **How will I uniquely identify each salesperson?**
>
> **What kinds of information will I need to maintain for each salesperson?**
>
> **What data type should I assign to each field?**

7. Add 5 records to the Salesperson Master table.
8. Create a report, sorted by salesperson, that calculates the total sales for each salesperson.

INDEPENDENT CHALLENGE 4

As the controller for Caselli & Montoya PCB's, a custom printed circuit board manufacturing company, it is your responsibility to evaluate and select various insurance plans that your employees can purchase at a discount. These various insurance plans include life, disability, health, dental, and vision insurance. Since each employee can tailor their plans to their own personal and family needs, you would like to create a report that details which plans each employee has elected to purchase, how much that coverage is costing each employee, and what their amount of coverage consists of. You have decided to create a database that includes two tables: the Employee Detail table and the Plan Master table.

1. Create a database called "C&M's Insurance Benefits".
2. Use the form provided below to assist you in planning the "Plan Master" table. This table will maintain information regarding what plans each employee has elected to purchase (such as their monthly rate and their amount of coverage):

How will I uniquely identify each plan?

What types of general information about each plan will I need to maintain?

What types of information will I need to calculate the cost and coverage for each plan?

Fields	Data Type	Primary Key

3. Enter 10 records into the Plan Master table. Be sure to enter at least two records for each kind of plan, such as a Standard Dental Plan and a Deluxe Dental Plan.
4. Use the form provided below to help you create the Employee Detail table. This table will contain information about the insurance plans themselves (such as the plan code, and plan description):

How will I uniquely identify each detail record?

What types of information will I need to track about the plans each employee has elected to purchase?

How will I calculate the total cost to each employee report their amounts of coverage under each insurance plan?

Fields	Data Type	Primary Key

5. Develop and enter 15 records for the Employee Detail table.
6. Create a report that shows which plans each employee has purchased, what their level of coverage under each plan is, and what the total monthly cost for each employee is.

Visual Workshop

Create a database named "Carpet Master" and the table or tables necessary to produce the report shown in Figure VW-1, then create and print the report.

FIGURE VW-1: **Customer Accounts Listing report**

Customer Accounts Listing

Type	Company	Last Name	First Name	Customer Since	Sales YTD
Commercial					
	A&M Auto			5/24/97	$3,750.00
	Acme Services			10/21/95	$12,000.00
	Angie's Temps			2/6/97	$4,300.00
	Butch's Meat Market			5/1/98	$1,200.00
	Cardiologists			6/11/97	$8,500.00
	Designs by David			8/3/97	$2,200.00
	E Street Offices			12/25/97	$11,750.00
	Hugh's Bakery			6/21/98	$1,500.00
	Vintage Apartments			10/17/97	$9,500.00
Sum					*$54,700.00*
Residential					
		Anderson	Joseph	4/25/98	$400.00
		Gomez	Barbara	7/30/97	$750.00
		Lucey	Angela	4/10/98	$600.00
		Martin	Teresa	2/27/98	$1,000.00
		Mirabelli	Albina	3/14/98	$800.00
		Ruhl	Bill	1/5/96	$1,200.00
Sum					*$4,750.00*
Grand Total					*$59,450.00*

Page 1 of 1

Index